STRIKING BACK

The Untold Story
of an Anti-Apartheid Striker

Mary Manning emigrated to Australia until her name had been forgotten by potential employers, who associated her with the 'anti-establishment' label. Now living and working in Dublin, she has given talks throughout Ireland, as well as in London, New York and Washington. She has two daughters.

Sinéad O'Brien is an award-winning filmmaker and author. Her non-fiction book *Left for Dead* was named *Sunday Times* Sports Book of the Year and shortlisted for the William Hill Sports Book Award.

 @strikingbackmm1

STRIKING BACK

The Untold Story
of an Anti-Apartheid Striker

Mary Manning
with Sinéad O'Brien

The Collins Press

First published in 2017 by
The Collins Press
West Link Park
Doughcloyne
Wilton
Cork
T12 N5EF
Ireland

Photographs courtesy Mary Manning unless otherwise credited.

Additional research and Writing Assistant: Cara Loftus

A CIP record for this book is available from the British Library.

Paperback ISBN: 978-1-84889-324-5

Typesetting by Patricia Hope
Typeset in Minion Pro

Printed in Poland by Białostockie Zakłady Graficzne SA

For Mam and Da

CONTENTS

'Never doubt that a small group of thoughtful, committed citizens can change the world. Indeed, it is the only thing that ever has.'

Margaret Mead

1

Ignorance is Bliss

Dublin, Ireland
19 July 1984

The day started like any other. I slept through my alarm only to be woken by Mam hollering loudly up the stairs of our house in Kilmainham.

'It took you long enough to get this job, Mary. Could you not try hanging on to it?'

This was Mam's favourite line, which really made no sense at all because, having started off part-time in Dunnes Stores, I had now worked there full-time for nearly two and a half years. With little interest in moving I slowly opened my eyes to find my two great loves staring down at me – Patch, my dog, who we'd got when I was eight years old, sitting protectively on the bed, and above her on the wall, Bruce Springsteen! Footsteps padded softly up the stairs and I smiled to myself – I knew it was my Da. He popped his head around the bedroom door and, out of earshot of Mam, whispered that if I got myself out of the bed quick enough he would make me a rasher sandwich. I was the youngest and only girl of three siblings and he still treated me like his baby. By the time I made it downstairs, Mam had already gone to her cleaning job and Da was putting the final touches to my breakfast. I grabbed it, ran out the front door and across the street to catch the No. 78 bus which brought me to the city centre. I normally enjoyed the quiet solitude of my short bus journey into work but the last few mornings had been filled with a sense of growing unease. A huge row was brewing between our union, the Irish Distributive Administrative Trade Union (IDATU), and the management of the Henry Street branch of Dunnes Stores where I worked. They were constantly at loggerheads over the ill treatment of the shopworkers; issues such as lack of toilet breaks, excessive disciplinary action over till receipts, unreasonable working hours and we had been trying to get a meeting with management for weeks but this new row was entirely different and escalating at a rate none of us had anticipated.

The general secretary of our union John Mitchell had handed down a directive instructing all IDATU members not to handle the sale of South African goods in their place of work. John Mitchell, fairly new to the job, was a Cork man with radical views. He was involved in the Irish Anti-Apartheid Movement and had been secretary in 1981 for the campaign against Irish Rugby team's tour of South Africa that year. IDATU was considered one of the most conservative unions in Ireland at the time and Mitchell's ideas were deemed new and unusual within the executive. In the beginning, they indulged the more harmless-looking motions, for example, the motion on apartheid. At that time it was fashionable to pass motions banning South African goods, and nobody would ever speak against it. The difference was that John Mitchell implemented the ban.

In reaction to this, our boss, Ben Dunne Jnr, the managing director of Dunnes Stores, instructed his management that all staff had to handle the sale of South African goods. In recent days, management in our branch in Henry Street had been summoning all IDATU shopworkers individually to the office and warning them that any refusal to sell the South African produce would be met with serious consequences, possibly even the loss of employment. Only the day beforehand my colleague Michelle Gavin had been let off with a final warning after she refused to register a sale.

Summer was unusually hot in Ireland that year and I was already sticky with sweat from the humid bus journey by the time I made it into the city centre. Walking over the Ha'penny Bridge, I paused to stare down the River Liffey, mentally gearing myself up for a day of work.

In the distance I saw Karen Gearon, our shop steward, and called out to her. As we sauntered towards Henry Street more shopworkers arrived from different directions and strolled along with us, all of us gossiping about the day ahead. By the time we reached the staff entrance to Dunnes, we all knew that today would be eventful. None of us was too worried, though.

John Mitchell, the general secretary of our union, IDATU, pictured here addressing an anti-apartheid rally in 1984 (© Derek Speirs).

In fact, the feeling amongst the thirty or so of us in the changing room was unusually chirpy that morning. This was 1984 and we were all young women so our conversations mainly revolved around hair. There was no such thing as hair too huge so perms, puffed-up styles and waves dominated much of conversation, both inside and outside work. But as the time approached to go out on the shop floor the chat turned to the day at hand. With the support of the union and this new directive we might finally have an opportunity to give a long overdue 'middle finger' to our boss, Ben Dunne, and his management.

The mouthy, cocksure attitude of the boisterous changing room evaporated as we entered the shop floor. I took my position at one of the tills as usual, but what was unusual was the line of managers standing behind us. There were so many of them; too many for them all to belong to our store. They had been drafted in from other branches to deal with this situation in a show of power.

Glancing up and down the line of cash registers I suddenly realised that every one of us put on the tills that morning was an IDATU member. The shop was beginning to fill with customers so it was only a matter of time before one of us would be tested. I was aware that, in comparison to other branches of the Dunnes Stores chain, the Henry Street branch had a particularly hostile relationship with their staff but what was happening here felt very heavy-handed and intimidating.

Immediately the mundane task of stacking shelves, which I normally despised, intensified in its appeal. My palms started sweating as I opened up my cash register. Everything after this happened very quickly. I spotted a middle-aged woman in the distance with two large yellow grapefruits in her basket. My heartbeat increased at the sight of them. I avoided eye contact and popped my head down straight away. 'Please don't come to me, please go to any other till,' I thought to myself, but the woman plonked her basket at my till, completely oblivious to the internal crisis unfolding within me. Politely, I informed her that because of an instruction from my union, which was opposed to the importation of goods produced under the apartheid regime, I was unable to register the sale of South African goods today.

The words just robotically stuttered out of my mouth – we had all been laughing so much when learning the line in the changing room I wasn't even sure I had said it right. It barely sounded like English! Before she even had a chance to respond, the manager behind me stepped forward and instructed that I go ahead with the sale. Clearly ruffled, the woman kindly offered to put them aside, explaining she had no idea they were South African. I hoped this might be the end of it – but no. Once again, the manager instructed me to register the sale of the grapefruits. I glanced around at the other tills but all heads were firmly faced downwards and I couldn't make eye contact with anyone. Unsure of what to do, again I refused. Immediately the manager told me to report the manager's office. There was a moment where nothing happened; the world stopped. All eyes were on me, and a silence hung in the air, only accentuated by the abrupt halt of the till operations. The customers, the managers and my co-workers all looked on in disbelief as I closed off my till. It suddenly occurred to me that I might really be on my own here. Yes, we'd all practised the lines in harmony, chanting in the changing room, but nobody thought about what happened after the words were uttered aloud. Nobody had thought this far ahead, because nobody really thought this would happen.

I was marched up to the manager's office and, to my relief, Karen Gearon swiftly stopped what she was doing and followed. Karen and I now sat in the manager's office. This woman was one of the toughest managers at Dunnes Stores, and the next few minutes were both uncomfortable and terrifying for me. I sat in a low seat, while the manager stood in front of us like a strict schoolteacher. She asked me if I fully understood the consequences of my actions, and then came the threat of suspension.

When her tactics didn't work, she tried to isolate me. She told Karen to leave the room and gave me five minutes to consider my decision. During this time she advised me to think long and hard about what I was about to do. She told me that, if I walked out of this store, I'd be blacklisted all over Dublin and I'd never work again. She also asked if I truly believed that any of my colleagues would be stupid enough to support me. But I knew she was wrong. This was a directive from our union and I was just following their instruction – I had support. I informed her my decision was final. I would be following the union directive and would not be handling the sale of South African goods. With that, she suspended me. When I came back down the stairs I saw that the shop floor was at a standstill; everyone was waiting to see what had happened. As the shopworkers stared up at me, I thought to myself, 'what if nobody else walks out? What if I'm on my own here?' As these thoughts raced through my mind, a wisp of relief arrived as Karen Gearon's booming voice sliced through the stony silence, instructing everyone to cease what they were doing. And that was it – the tills were abandoned, the aisles deserted and half-emptied boxes were left discarded on the shop floor. With that, we all marched out in unison.

There must have been twenty-five of us outside the shop and the jokes were flying as we watched our managers through the shop window, struggling with the tills and the menial tasks normally undertaken by us. But by lunchtime I could feel a change of mood. It was small and gradual, but the initial high was waning and nerves were beginning to fray.

The anxieties set in shortly after this. People began to break away from the main group and huddle in smaller ones. Private chats and nervous glances were followed by a small yet increasingly noticeable drop in numbers. In fear of losing their jobs many of the staff were drifting back to work. On one level, I could sympathise with their anxieties about losing a job, but a larger part of me was concerned I'd be left out here on my own. Later that afternoon a much-needed boost arrived in the form of Tommy Davis when he turned up for his shift at about 4.30 p.m. Tommy worked out the back of the shop taking in deliveries and stacking shelves on the evening shift. Once he saw there was a picket line, that was it – he wouldn't cross it. He promptly joined us and although we were down in numbers, our spirits were lifted. But by close of business we were down to just nine of us – eight women and one man. This was the moment we became known as the Dunnes Stores Strikers.

*   *   *

They say ignorance is bliss and in those very early days of the strike this truly was the case. It would be easy to say now, after the fact, that our action had sprung from a deep-rooted concern for the inhumane system in South Africa, but the reality was quite different. On that morning of 19 July 1984, if anybody had asked me or any of the other strikers how to spell the word 'apartheid' let alone explain its meaning, we wouldn't have known where to begin. A news blackout had been implemented by the South African government so we, like most people in Ireland, knew very little about what was really going on there. We were working-class kids with very little education, who simply viewed the day's happenings as a brief diversion from the mundane. The summer of '84 was a blistering one, the hottest on record for nearly twenty years, so, assured by our union representative Brendan Archbold that the whole matter would be resolved quickly, we decided a few days on a picket line was an exciting alternative to working in a stifling shop with high-handed managers 'lording it' over us. We were young and nearly all of us lived at home with our parents so the loss of a few days' wages wasn't going to kill us.

On that first day, 19 July, we hung around on the pavement on Henry Street outside Dunnes Stores long after the lights of the shop had been dimmed, the nine of us huddled together. Our nervous laughter and continuous chatter bounced against the evening silence. The rest of the staff with bowed heads had passed by us earlier on their way home. The mood was relatively positive and there was talk of going for drinks but as the summer sun dipped into the horizon I realised I had to get home. Returning over the Ha'penny Bridge towards the bus stop to take me home I was blissfully unaware that my refusal to register the sale of those two yellow Outspan grapefruits had already set off an unstoppable chain of events. Little did we know the battle was only just beginning.

Obviously, I couldn't have foreseen any of this on that fateful day. As I stepped off the bus, my main concern was contemplating what to tell Mam and Da, especially Mam. How was I going to tell her that I had just been suspended? There was no way she was going to take this well. As the bus pulled away I caught a glimpse of my sole pillar of support: Patch was standing at the front gate of my house, guarding it like her life depended on it. Catching sight of me, she bounded down the footpath and up into my arms, like she did every evening on my return home from work. By the time I reached the front door I decided it was probably best not to mention that it was my suspension that had started the dispute. Just assure Mam that it was a bit of mix-up and that I would be back to work before the end of the week. I'd just keep quiet and wait out the week. Then I'd be back in work, back on the tills, back to normal.

Of course, this never happened.

2

Without Good Reason

I was born at home on 8 July 1963 in Kilmainham to Kevin and Josephine Manning. Back then, Kilmainham was very much a working-class area in Dublin city and the houses on my street reflected this – we lived in a two-up two-down, originally with an outside toilet. When I come along, after my older brothers Brian and Lar, Mam and Da partitioned off their bedroom to make a small bedroom for me.

The Manning household was, for the most part, a happy house and I can always remember from a very early age that complaining or moaning was always greeted by Mam pointing out how lucky we all were.

'We mightn't have much but we have enough,' she would tell us.

Mam was one of those people who always sought out the good in a situation and in people, no matter what. Unlike Mam, who could talk for Ireland, Da was a man of very few words. In fact, he rarely spoke unless he had something important to say, and this would often be demonstrated if he truly believed a person or people had been

My parents, Kevin and Josephine Manning, on their wedding day, 20 April 1960.

wronged in some way. Da had amazing compassion and sympathy for the underdog. He also had a highly accurate intuition for when something was right or wrong and could easily break down for myself and my brothers why the conventional way of judging situations wasn't always the fairest.

'No one loses a day's wages and stands in the bitter cold without a good reason,' he once told me.

Etched in my mind is a vivid memory of the very day my Da said these words to me. It was Christmas Eve 1972 and I was walking up a bustling O'Connell Street, teeming with shoppers, my nine-year-old hand gripped in his.

It was a wet day and eventually we were forced to take shelter at the entrance of a butcher's shop. As we huddled in with other shoppers also avoiding the downpour, the heavy odour of raw meat wafted up my nostrils and a wave of nausea washed over me. I pressed my face into Da's coat and listened to the rain bucketing down on to the red-and-white striped canvas above my head, willing it to cease. Today was

(L–r): My brothers, Lar and Brian, and me in 1964.

a very important day. I was getting new shoes – not just any old pair – no hand-me-downs from a cousin or second-hand ones from a neighbour or friend – I was getting brand spanking new ones. This was a very rare occurrence in the Manning household or any house on our street for that matter. My thoughts were solely focused on two exciting prospects – Santa was coming tomorrow, and I would be opening my presents in new shoes.

The rain wasn't easing off but more time had passed than I had patience for so I tugged the arm of Da's coat – no reaction. Annoyed by his lack of response, I tugged

A school photo of a six-year-old me.

harder. It was only when I looked up and followed his eyeline that I realised he was transfixed by some sort of commotion taking place across the street from us. A group of people, maybe twenty or twenty-five men and women of all ages, were walking in a kind of circle at the main entrance of a large department store. Many of them were holding big signs. I squinted but from where I stood I was unable to read what they said. I soon found myself more and more drawn to a man, older than the others, who had stepped away from the group and begun speaking into a megaphone. I heard him bellow things like 'workers' rights' and 'fair pay' but it was impossible for my nine-year-old self to decipher any proper meaning of what was being said. Instead, all I kept thinking was would somebody not get this old man a cup of hot tea or at the very least an umbrella? He was completely drenched, soaked to the bone.

'What are they doing?' I asked my Da.

Before he could answer I heard an irritated voice from amongst the crowd.

'They're lucky to have a job at all – they should get back to work,' a man declared, with vexation in his voice.

Other voices, men and woman, all seemingly equally disgruntled began to sound off in agreement.

'They're an absolute disgrace to themselves and their families.'

At first Da said nothing but I could see the upset rise in his face.

'They are on strike, Mary,' he told me, and then raising his voice over the drone of mounting disapproval, he said. 'No one loses a day's pay to stand in the bitter cold without a very good reason.'

Although my main preoccupation that rainy Christmas Eve was to get to the top of O'Connell Street and into the shoe shop where my new shoes awaited, I felt a great sense of pride at how my Da had managed to silence the crowd. In my young mind, Da was right.

That was the first and the last I heard of any kind of workers' strike until the summer of 1980. By then I was seventeen years old and had just left school, enjoying that new-found sense of freedom that comes with having a part-time job and the knowledge that I would never have to cross my school gates again. *Dallas* was gracing our screens, the soundtracks to *Fame* and *The Blues Brothers* were blaring from our radios and the Cold War between the Soviet Union and the West was at its height.

On holidays at Butlins.
I am aged about nine.

Neither of my parents was overtly political: I would describe them as people who had a great moral compass but there was never any great political conversation at the Manning dinner table. All of that changed for a time in August 1980 when we, like the rest of the world, became utterly gripped by the events unfolding at a shipyard in Gdansk, Poland. The Communist Soviet government had just announced new economic austerity policies for the already beleaguered and financially strained Polish people, and workers at the Lenin Shipyard exploded in anger. After years of impoverishment and suppression this was their tipping point. Led by Lech Wałęsa, this strike played out over several weeks and at nine o'clock each evening the television in our living room became the focal point for the whole family. For the first time in my life I felt truly affected by the plight of others.

The effect was profound – it was in this moment I began to gain an understanding of people power and how sometimes, just sometimes, it can lead to change on a level that no one could have predicted. In those few weeks the breezy soundtrack of the Western world was pushed into the background as the voices of a long-suffering Polish nation revolted against their oppressors, winning the right to organise their own non-governmental union – their voices so powerful they simply could not be ignored.

The 1980s was a time of complete upheaval for the ordinary worker. Once-powerful unions were coming under increasing pressure from a new world order that wanted to bulldoze a path for the capitalist era. As Cold War fears and austerity measures dominated society and with Margaret Thatcher's government controlling Britain, the next strike to capture imaginations was the miners' strike in the UK, which had begun a few months before ours, in March 1984. We in Ireland seemed particularly affected by the crushing and humiliation of the miners and for many it reminded us of the imperialist oppression the country had suffered under British rule. Although our own strike at Dunnes Stores was embryonic it would soon be intertwined with that of the miners – very soon we would be reaching to each other for support.

I went to bed far earlier than normal the day the Dunnes Stores strike started – I thought it wise to avoid Mam. I had toyed with the idea of telling Da what was going on at work but then decided against. He would give me his support, but I knew that he would feel obliged to tell Mam. After weighing it up I decided it was probably best to hold off and see how the next day panned out. Like everything else, this didn't go according to plan. By the time I was up and dressed the next morning, a news report announced on the radio that a worker from Dunnes Stores on Henry Street had been suspended for refusing to handle the sale of two South African Outspan grapefruits. It was apparently only a small piece at the end of the bulletin but Mam, Da and my two older brothers, Lar and Brian, were all intrigued as to why I had made no mention of it.

To this day, I will never forget the look on Mam's face when she realised that the worker who had refused to handle the sale of the grapefruit and had been suspended was me. Her hand went to her mouth and as she sat down I could see a look of fear seep into her face.

'Please tell me, Mary ...' She then hesitated as if for effect. '... Please tell me that you haven't gone out on strike.'

My silence told her everything she didn't want to hear.

'Jesus, Mary and Joseph, would somebody talk some sense into this girl?' I knew this was bad – Mam, a deeply religious woman, who went to Mass every single day rarely took the Lord's name in vain.

Da, as always, remained calm but he had questions too. How many of us had gone out on strike? Why were we out on strike for something that had nothing to do with us? My eldest brother, Lar, said nothing. He was the quiet one and we were very close. Brian, on the other hand, always had something to say, especially if it got me into hot water. Since before I could even walk or talk we had fought like cats and dogs.

'Out on strike for load of people you've never even met.' He couldn't control his amusement at my predicament. 'Only you, Mary. You're one in a million!'

I wanted to deck him but at this stage I had a far bigger battle on my hands. Mam was livid and even Da, who I thought I could count on for support, looked very apprehensive. I didn't want to admit that only nine of us had stayed out – I was sure this would send Mam over the edge. Instead I decided to explain that the 'grapefruit situation' was just the tipping point for everything else that was going on with Dunnes Stores management – the low pay, their ill-treatment of lower-ranking staff like us – but as the words fell from my mouth, even I was beginning to start some internal questioning. Why were we not on strike for these reasons?

As I stood in the kitchen facing questions from my family, the political situation in South Africa seemed very detached from my reality. I felt claustrophobic and knew I had to get out and away from my family, especially Mam. The distraught look on her face was driving me mad and right now I couldn't deal with the drama. I quickly assured everyone that this was a storm in a teacup, it would blow over in a matter of days, possibly even by the end of today, and I had to run or I'd miss my bus. With that, I was gone.

As I crossed over the Ha'penny Bridge and walked towards the turn for Henry Street it felt I was entering a gateway to a whole new and unknown reality. Everything looked the same but felt utterly different, like an alternate universe that held echoes of a previous world.

Henry Street was, and still is, one of the commercial hubs in Dublin city. North of the River Liffey, it has never had the glamour of the more affluent shopping streets in the upper middle class southside. For me, from a working-class area, there was something cold, bordering judgemental, on those streets: you couldn't walk down them without feeling like an outsider. But Henry Street felt like home. What it lacked in glamour it made up for, in abundance, with scents, colour and character. The familiar lyrical shouts of 'three for a pound' and 'get your strawberries' reverberating around the streets greeted you each day. There were stalls full of flowers, fruit, vegetables – an explosion of colour and sound as you walked through Moore Street Market, where the back entrance to Dunnes Stores is. Everybody here was their own character – weather-beaten faces, leathery hands, wrinkles etched like stories across their faces. Here people knew you, they told you stories, they made you laugh and they welcomed you. Here you felt at home.

As the entrance to Dunnes Stores came into sight my spirits were immediately lifted as I was greeted by the sound of Liz and Alma convulsed with laughter. Soon I was too, when Alma showed me that under her clothes she was wearing a bikini.

'If we're gonna be out for the next few days I'm not missing out on this heatwave,' she told me. Alma, the ultimate sun worshipper, never missed a trick.

Everyone else had arrived early and there was a giddy excitement in the air – the kind of feeling you have when heavy snow or frozen pipes result in an unexpected day off school. As we huddled together, the laughs kept coming thick and fast, particularly when Tommy, the only man who had stayed out on strike, asked for first dibs on Alma's bikini when she'd had enough sun. As shop opening time drew closer the laughs slowly turned to nervous giggles and the conversations turned to focus on what was ahead of us. Apart from a few hours the day before, none of us had even stood on a picket line, let alone run one.

There was a great sense of relief when we caught sight of our union rep, Brendan Archbold, walking towards us with placards for us that read 'Irish Distributive Administrative Trade Union. OFFICIAL TRADE DISPUTE'. A bit older and far more politicised than any of us, Brendan Archbold was a man we all knew well and greatly respected. In the two and a half years I had worked in Dunnes Stores I had watched him spar relentlessly with the draconian system in which Dunnes Stores operated.

In the store, we were treated coldly and cruelly. There were rules that we had to abide by or face disciplinary action, some of which were so uncompromising they would often prove impossible to adhere to. Issues such as the lack of toilet breaks and incorrect till receipts caused the biggest problems. There were ten cash registers in the Henry Street branch and if you were on a register you had to put your name on a list for what they called a 'relief'. 'Relief' was a member of staff who would take over your register while you went the bathroom – but there was only ever one person relieving the registers. If you were last on the list you had to wait until every person before you had gone up and back. When you finally did get to go to the toilet, you would often have the humiliation of a male manager following and timing you from outside the door. Even though the staff toilet was three floors up from the shop floor, any staff member who took longer than the three minutes allocated for a toilet break could be disciplined. Even if you were pregnant or ill, no allowances were made on this rule. In spite of the long hours on the cash registers without breaks, there was continual questioning and disciplining over till receipts, which could easily go wrong due to exhaustion after a ten-hour shift – if you went more than £1 over, it went on your record. There were other more trivial issues that bothered us, such as being forbidden to speak to any other worker while we were on the tills – even to the girls sitting beside us. During working hours we couldn't call each other by our first names; it had to be 'Miss' or 'Mr'.

This attitude permeated from the top down. One day I was horrified to witness a senior Dunnes Stores board member, while inspecting the store, wiping their finger along an aisle and then simply wiping the dirt on a manager's jacket. While this particular manager treated us appallingly on a daily basis, in that moment, as he held his head down in fear-filled shame, I felt sorry for him. This poisonous treatment of staff continued down the ladder, ending with us. Brendan Archbold was the antithesis of this management which lacked any form of compassion. He was a complete rarity in the male-dominated world of the 1980s in that he genuinely treated everybody equally. Whether you were male, female, young or old, he was a man who always had time not only to listen but to act quickly to rectify a situation. Anybody who worked the more menial jobs in Dunnes benefited from his unwavering perseverance for their rights and for that reason, he had the complete trust of every one of us on the picket line.

Brendan Archbold, IDATU official and our union representative at Dunnes Stores, Henry Street (© Derek Speirs).

The first thing Brendan did was give us all a crash course on how to run a picket. There were two customer entrances: the main one to the front of the shop and a smaller one to the side. There was the delivery door to the back of the shop just off Moore Street. This was where all the lorry and van deliveries were made, including those from South Africa – and these were the deliveries we were trying to stop. Every entrance needed to be manned during opening hours, which included a late night on Thursdays. The front entrance was the busiest point of entry, so was therefore the best place to dissuade customers and possibly even other workers from crossing the picket line. There were all sorts of laws that had to be adhered to when picketing, which Brendan then went through with us – no noise nuisance, use of threatening language or offensive material, libel or slander in leaflets, banners, placards, chants or speeches. Also, and most importantly, while on the picket line, we had to keep walking up and down. There could be no stopping and absolutely no picketing beyond the perimeter of the entrance of Dunnes Stores – this was strictly forbidden.

As I listened, a lucid image of the first strike I had witnessed, as a child, with my Da, entered my head. Protesting workers circling the main entrance of another large department store only a few streets away from where I stood now. I also remembered how those other shoppers had spoken about them with disdain. I had to hope that by now more people looked upon strikes with Da's understanding view rather than a judgemental one. Besides, those strikers had been out there for weeks. I wasn't sure why we would need to worry about all these rules. At this stage, we were all staring at each other, and I knew every one of us was thinking the same thing – why would any of this apply to us? We were only going to be out here for a couple of days.

As the crash course was coming to an end our union head, John Mitchell, arrived with words of encouragement. Until the previous day when we had all descended on his office I had never laid eyes on this man before and doubted any of the other strikers had either. However, this was a person that Brendan clearly respected and had time for so for that reason alone we immediately placed our trust in him. He was headstrong in his approach and made no bones about his beef with Dunnes Stores and its managing director.

Their challenged relationship was common knowledge amongst all of the IDATU members. John Mitchell spoke about the autocratic nature of Ben Dunne, his disregard for the union and South African politics. He told us that Dunnes Stores were getting high-quality fruit

On the picket line (l–r): Myself, Michelle Gavin, Sandra Griffin and Alma Russell: only a couple of days into the strike, with still no idea where it would lead (© Derek Speirs).

and vegetables at a cheap price and that they had no intention of bringing a halt to that.

Although I had never met Ben Dunne, I, like everyone who worked for Dunnes Stores, had heard all the stories about his legendary mood swings. Apparently you never quite knew which Ben Dunne you were going to meet until he entered the room. While clearly an astute businessman, he also had a reputation for being unpredictable in his temper, his decision-making and his attitude – and Mitchell, who had had dealings with him, went on to tell us some quite hilarious stories of Ben Dunne's erratic nature. Laughter broke out amongst us when John described a recent meeting, which opened with Ben Dunne angrily berating both the union and John personally, then promptly asking if he would like a cup of tea and inquiring how his family were doing.

The picture being painted here was one of a man with whom you always had to be on your guard because you never knew when he was likely to turn.

I felt what John Mitchell was doing that morning, first and foremost, before the shop door had even opened, was selling a situation to us. He was full of praise for our actions against the selling of South African produce and told us that other unions would come forward with support very soon – not to mention people in high places. We now understood that support from other unions meant that food companies and their delivery drivers would refuse to pass our picket – even for us, wet behind the ears, this was a no-brainer. No goods to sell equalled huge losses for Dunnes Stores. John's words were effective and to the point – he ended by telling us, in no uncertain terms, that the only way to get Dunnes to meet any of our demands was to hit them where it hurt – in the pocket.

3

A Line in the Sand

Despite the laughs, the blistering sunshine and being away from the toxic atmosphere that gripped the shop floor of Dunnes Stores, I didn't enjoy that morning on the picket line one bit. Our initial task was to try and dissuade other workers, basically our colleagues, from passing our picket. If that didn't work we were to call them 'scabs' – a derogatory term, centuries old, used against anybody who was considered to be a strike-breaker. In my mind this all felt a bit strange – many of those who had gone back into work were my friends and, in reality, I had no beef with any of them. They were in the same boat as all of us outside with regard to bad pay and ill treatment. My beef was with Dunnes Stores management and Ben Dunne.

Although my heart wasn't really in this name-calling – it's not what I thought I had signed up for! – I did what was asked of me, but I found it stressful and soon even the cooing of the ever-present pigeons was doing my head in. By mid-morning when my tea break came around I felt nothing but relief. The Dunnes staff canteen, where I'd spent over two years' worth of breaks, was right above where I marched. Obviously, this was a no-go zone for us strikers, so I wandered into the Kylemore Café a few doors down. Tommy Davis was sitting alone and I asked if I could join him. I hardly knew Tommy but I liked what I did know of him. He was a kind and gentle man who always wore a friendly smile on his face. We chatted, sipping tea, and were joined a few minutes later by Theresa Mooney. I knew Theresa vaguely as she worked in the cash office upstairs and I used to talk to her when I went up for change. It was a bizarre scenario, the three of us barely knowing each other, suddenly thrown into a situation where we were fighting this battle together. We joked initially, but soon we fell silent as the atmosphere became tense.

Theresa finally broke the silence, admitting that while she would never pass a picket she wondered what would happen next. My admiration for Theresa's determination grew in that moment; working in the cash office meant she herself would never even come into contact with South African produce so it would have been very easy for her to go back inside. Unlike me, she didn't have the luxury of living at home. Although only twenty-two, she had recently married and was living in a mobile home while she and her husband, Brendan, saved for their first mortgage. Two other strikers – Cathryn O'Reilly and Vonnie Monroe – were both single mothers. I felt physically ill thinking about the hardships these women might face and I had to admit to Tommy and Theresa that I was grateful for all the support, but I really hoped this wasn't something unachievable that we'd lose our jobs over. This is when Tommy stepped in as a source of reassurance, and in an instant relieved my fears. This was a union issue, he assured us, and we were following orders so it wasn't up to us to worry how to fix it – that's what the union was for. By the time our tea break ended Tommy had managed to quell the majority of our fears. I still dreaded confronting my colleagues at the end of the day but I vowed to stay focused and, armed with my new frame of mind, I returned to the picket.

The next few hours passed somewhat successfully and as morning turned to early afternoon I was beginning to get the hang of how to explain what the strike was about without messing it up too much. People's reactions were very much a mixed bag. A few, who fully understood our predicament at being forced to handle the sale of African goods, didn't pass the picket. Others gave support more grudgingly, probably out of embarrassment at passing a picket line rather than really caring what we were striking about. But the majority of customers just brushed passed us before we could even explain properly, some even suggesting we give recommendations of somewhere else they could get their shopping so cheap before preaching about the impoverished in South Africa. Our real obstacle was beginning to surface as the day went on – Dunnes Stores had the cheap-goods end of the market completely sewn up and in recession-hit Ireland that was going to be difficult for us to compete with. (It would be another thirteen years before Tesco opened in Ireland, with Aldi following two years later and Lidl the year after that.)

Karen, Liz and myself were buoyed by a conversation we got into with an elderly lady who was horrified by our predicament. Riding on the wave of this rare show of support Karen became quite animated as she described in detail how Ben Dunne had told us we either handle the South African produce or find new jobs.

'Shame on that awful man,' she said, in disbelief. 'You should be proud of yourselves, sticking up for your rights against a bully.'

We thanked her profusely and asked that she tell all her family and friends.

'Of course I will. It's a disgrace,' she said. 'I wouldn't touch the stuff either. Not after a nigger had touched it.'

And with that she meandered off down the street with her empty shopping basket, leaving us to wonder had we actually heard her correctly. Of course, we had.

As afternoon drifted into early evening I could feel the muscles in my calves begin to tighten. My arms were also killing me from carrying the placard – all this walking and talking was exhausting. Leaning against a pillar, I let my face bask in the hot afternoon sun. The well-deserved moment of tranquillity was suddenly broken by something wet landing on my head. It felt too big for a raindrop so I reckoned it must have been one of those cooing pigeons that couldn't seem to get enough of us. I looked upwards but the clear sky was empty. Alma was also looking upwards with the same puzzled look on her face as I had on mine. I caught her eye and in that instant we both knew there was something more sinister at play. No way could two pigeons plan and execute a simultaneous bowel movement.

(L–r): My brother Lar and me at my twenty-first birthday party, in 1984, ten days before the strike.

I reached for my head and I picked out what looked like the remains of cooked tomato from my hair. That's when we heard giggling – sure enough, some of our colleagues on their afternoon break were throwing food down on our heads. They kept their faces hidden but the next thing we heard was 'Nigger lovers'.

My jaw dropped in disbelief. We knew that our colleagues who had gone back inside would have come under immediate pressure to alienate themselves from us. But this behaviour was at a level I could never have anticipated. These were supposed friends of mine, many of whom had attended my twenty-first birthday party just the week beforehand. Any guilt I had been harbouring about calling my colleagues names instantly evaporated. When I heard Alma hollering, 'Show your faces, scabs!', I immediately joined her in what swiftly became a swear-driven slagging match between the picket line and the girls in the canteen – on a scale of aggression I had never heard before. We only ceased and dispersed when we saw two gardaí turning onto Henry Street and Karen Gearon quickly reminded us that that verbal abuse was illegal.

We began recircling the picket line, enraged, but also unexpectedly invigorated by what had just taken place. We now couldn't wait until the end of the workday when we could confront out colleagues face to face. I wondered when visible if they would be so open and frank in their racist abuse. One thing was for certain though, above anything else, a line in the sand had been drawn between 'us' and 'them' and I wondered when we returned to work if things could be the same.

* * *

Nearly everything that happened during those first few days on the picket line was alien to us all, but what happened at the end of our first week brought our journey into the unknown to a new pinnacle. John Mitchell's promise that support would be forthcoming from people in 'high places' arrived late Saturday afternoon in the form of Kader Asmal. He was accompanied by his wife, Louise, and what looked like a presidential press corps. Without any notice at all they descended on the picket line – journalists from all the major Irish publications and even a news crew wanting to report our action on the national evening news. Until that moment, none of us had ever heard of Kader Asmal but as we listened to him address the journalists we very quickly learned that if there was anybody we needed supporting us,

Kader Asmal was the man. He was not only the founding member and chief executive of the Irish Anti-Apartheid Movement (IAAM), he was a man who moved in very powerful circles.

Born in South Africa, Kader Asmal was the son of a shopkeeper in a small rural town, Stanger, fifty miles or so north of Durban. He was a third-generation South African, a member of the Indian community that had been established in Natal as a workforce for the sugar plantations during the nineteenth century.

According to Kader Asmal, the transformative moment in his political understanding occurred when footage of Nazi concentration camp victims was shown to him. He gradually saw a link between this tragedy in European history and his own country under apartheid. Although he had qualified as a teacher in the early 1950s, he soon decided on a career in law in order to oppose the regime. While teaching, Kader obtained a BA degree through the University of South Africa and in 1959 travelled to London to study law. In that same year he founded the British Anti-Apartheid Movement. Prohibited from returning to the land of his birth because of his political activities, in 1964 he moved to Ireland to take up an appointment as a law lecturer specialising in human rights, labour and international law at Trinity College Dublin and it was very soon after this that he founded the IAAM.

A short, bespectacled man, Kader chain-smoked his way through the press conference.

'We have waited for twenty years for this kind of action against the South African regime – and it has been worthwhile,' he said, without an ounce of restraint in his voice. 'I commend Mary Manning and all of her colleagues for what they are doing.'

The atmosphere became nothing short of electric as Kader cajoled and pushed his agenda strongly with the press. To be honest, standing there, hearing him list off hard facts and figures relating to the horrendous atrocities that had befallen the black South African people under apartheid rule, I felt like a bit of a fraud, like someone who was about to sit an exam they had never studied for. I had heard

Kader Asmal at an anti-apartheid meeting in Dublin 1984, where he asked the Irish government and the public to boycott South African goods (© Derek Speirs).

some of what he was relating to the journalists before – the imprisonment of Nelson Mandela and the brutal murder of Steve Biko – but as far as the rest was concerned, every single bit of it was news to me and the other strikers.

Kader fielded questions from the press with the confidence of a seasoned politician, for fundamentally this is what he was. Photographs were taken of all of us with Kader, some of us with Kader, then Kader and me. It seemed that there were more photographs taken than could fill several newspapers for a year. As quickly as he had appeared, Kader was gone again. I don't think any of us on the picket line had ever before witnessed anyone or experienced anything quite so flamboyant and energetic in our lives.

That night as I lay in bed, a maelstrom of thoughts swam around my head – so much had happened in the last few days, it was hard to keep up. That day a member of the IAAM had given us some literature about South Africa and apartheid, so high on my list was to study this and visit my local library to find out more about the issue we were actually striking about. What I had heard from Kader Asmal that afternoon, limited as it was, had left me with an urgent desire to know more.

Later that night, Da popped his head around the door with Patch, who immediately jumped up on the bed beside me.

'How did the week go?' Da asked me gently. Unlike Mam, his voice didn't carry the accusatory tone that hers did these days.

'Not bad, thanks, Da,' I assured him. 'Kader Asmal of the Irish Anti-Apartheid Movement, no less, came down to support us today.'

He looked impressed. I wanted to keep things this way so I didn't bother telling him how most things had played out during the week, in particular the dreadful hostilities that were escalating between us and our 'colleagues' who, it turned out, had no issue whatsoever about calling us 'nigger lovers' to our faces. If it hadn't been for Brendan Archbold's steadying presence on the picket line, I swear it would already have descended into a fist fight between 'us' and 'them' on several occasions. Da looked tired and a bit stressed and I hated seeing him this way.

'And you, Da, are you okay?' I asked.

'Ah sure I'm grand, Mary,' he said, but then he stepped inside the door and lowered his voice to a whisper. I felt immediately worried.

'I wouldn't say this in front of your Mam, but I really think you're doing the right thing, Mary. It's just her nerves, she worries so much about all of you kids.'

I felt suddenly overwhelmed. This was the first time in all my life I had heard my Da saying anything out loud that he didn't want me to share with my Mam – they were inseparable. I was so grateful for his support but also felt bad for upsetting Mam because I knew the pressure this exerted on Da. Mam was a real homemaker – she loved her house and her three children, but most of all she loved my Da. She herself had suffered a difficult childhood, and I always knew instinctively that this experience had pushed her to guard what she now, as an adult, had in her life. The downside to this need to protect us all, particularly as we got older, was that sometimes it felt more claustrophobic than helpful. I think it bothered me more so than the others and because of this the relationship between me and Mam hadn't always been easy. The reality was, this unforeseen strike was now testing our relationship in a way it had never been before.

'It'll be okay, Da, I promise you,' I said hopefully, even though I think we both knew this was a promise I might not be in a position to keep.

Da then smiled his soft reassuring smile, the one that over the years had helped me through trying times, and in that moment I really believed it was going to be okay. Next week was going to be a good week. Other unions would begin to show their hands by supporting us, the public would then back us and the Irish government would have no choice but to do the same. Dunnes Stores management would then have to follow suit – and in my mind this could not come soon enough.

When Da had left the room I snuggled up to Patch and fiddled with my hair. I felt something sticky and looked to find a dried-up tomato pip between my fingers that a long shower had not managed to remove. I felt enraged at my co-workers inside Dunnes Stores and couldn't wait to get back to the picket line to tell them exactly what I thought of their repulsive behaviour towards us – they were Scabs with a capital S!

4

Doubts Grow

The next week started off unexpectedly well. Sandra Griffin, a co-worker who had been on holidays the previous week, arrived to work on Monday morning. We watched her walking up Henry Street, wondering what she would do. Would she, like the others, cross the picket line and return to work, or would she stay out with us? Without hesitation, Sandra joined the picket, and although it was a small moment in the greater scheme of things it felt like a huge victory for us. We were now ten!

Another situation was also developing that morning on the picket line that caused a further flurry of excitement. It became quickly apparent that I had not been the only striker left more curious about apartheid and South Africa after Kader Asmal's appearance on the picket line. We had all spent our one day off asking questions and searching for answers. Now armed with individual findings, each one of us had something to offer as we embarked on an exercise to try and paint a clearer picture of what we were actually striking about. What emerged was pretty unpalatable for all of us.

Apartheid, literally 'apartness', was and is a process of racial segregation. It is fundamentally a system that defines people by one thing only: the colour of their skin. Race had been an issue for centuries in South Africa, with black South Africans increasingly subordinated, but the introduction of apartheid laws in 1948 brought their status to an all-time low. Under this new regime black South Africans were denied all basic human rights: the right to vote, the right to own land, the right to an education, the right to work in any sector other than that of manual labour. Each law was explicitly designed to downgrade people of colour and any resistance to this regime was met with immediate and brutal punishment: torture, banishment, life in prison, the death penalty or, in many cases, unexplained and unjustified death at the hands of the cruel South African police. Nelson Mandela and Steve Biko were prime, very public, examples.

The picture in front of us was still a hazy one and far from complete, but what had happened in these few hours on the picket line, five days into our strike, was defining. We as a group of people, for the first time, completely removed ourselves from own situation and our own problems and began to consider the suffering others were experiencing daily. What we successfully drew from this spirited and lively discussion was a moment of camaraderie and a small glimpse of what could be possibly be achieved if we put our minds together. I felt proud of us. The previous week, our main concern had been our hours of work, or maybe even for some of us whether our perm was set correctly. Now, though, we were investigating international moral questions and opening our eyes to the wider world. I felt like we had really achieved something and, although I didn't know it then, we had awakened our social and political consciences.

Our moment of glory was cut short after lunch when Brendan Archbold arrived on the picket line with a much-anticipated update. He assured us that support was still being rallied from other unions and was forthcoming, but Brendan also had other news. A meeting he and John had attended that morning in the union head office revealed that many of the executives within our union, IDATU, were not quite as enthusiastic about our action as the chief executive, John Mitchell. This had resulted in a stand-off between them about the issue. Brendan explained that many of these committee executives were older and very conservative and while they had agreed to authorise strike pay of £21 per week for all of us, they would not endorse any further action, namely an all-out strike. We had never really expected an all-out strike but the news that people in our own union were so indifferent to our action didn't do much to steady our confidence.

There was much we didn't understand but in the hours that followed a clearer picture began to reveal itself, one that told us we were part of a far more complex situation than we could have anticipated. John Mitchell, a hugely politicised and forward-thinking man, had pushed the anti-apartheid directive through his executive without anybody in the union really taking it seriously and apparently with some of them not even noticing. It was an action to make a point that 'issues of conscience' should be recognised in the workplace, but was never meant be the cause of any kind of strike. IDATU represented thousands of shopworkers around Ireland in department stores like Arnotts and Roches Stores. When they issued the directive to companies around the country that their workers 'could no longer handle the sale of South African goods' most shops agreed, knowing that their staff probably would not bother adhering to the directive, or that those who did would be so few that the impact on business would be minimal. The management in many of these stores were either allowing the staff to refuse or turning a blind eye to what was happening. The fact was that if management in our store had done likewise in those first few days we would have been back at work, the whole story forgotten. To be honest, until the directive was issued, I had no idea what was or wasn't South African produce on our shelves, and neither had anybody else on the picket line. The reality was that we had all been unwittingly selling the produce for months, even years.

The only company in Ireland that objected outright to the directive was Dunnes Stores, but even at that, the only shop in their chain that enforced the action at any real level was the Henry Street branch. The catalyst here was a toxic relationship between the management and staff. The truth of the matter was that when this directive was introduced, nobody, not even John Mitchell himself, had expected any shopworker in any store in Ireland to act on it. Unbeknownst to us when we walked out the door of Dunnes, there was nothing in place to deal with this eventuality. I had to admit to thinking that the words of flattery from John Mitchell as to how brave our action was were beginning to ring quite hollow now.

By the middle of the week we were hearing all sorts of rumours on the picket line – none of which gave us any reassurances whatsoever. Dunnes Stores management were refusing to comment publicly on our action, but word travelled fast that they regarded us as 'a bunch of silly young girls with too much time on their hands'. Although there was also a man on strike, Tommy Davis, the use of this language, referring to us 'as a bunch of silly young girls' was fully intended to undermine us and implant the notion that we were under the influence of a greater power, our union. Ben Dunne's hatred of unions was Thatcher-like. It was widely known, even by us, that he considered them nothing but a curse when trying to run a business and again gossip was rife that he was delighting in this opportunity to take on the unions and possibly even break them. It seemed to us now that we were possibly caught in the middle of something far bigger. Both Dunnes Stores management and John Mitchell, the general secretary of our union, had bigger agendas and neither was about to give in.

Another few days passed and the support that had been promised had not yet materialised, something that was beginning to play on everybody's nerves. Gradually, taking turns sunbathing out the back of the shop felt more of an obligation than a bit of craic as the hopes of ever returning to work ebbed away. The media attention that Kader Asmal had brought to the picket line had died away, quickly delivering something different in its wake. We noticed that certain sections of the media were now starting to refer both to us and the strike in negative terms, such as 'anarchists', 'lefties' and 'militant'. My name, as the person who started the whole dispute, kept cropping up far more than the others, which was not helping my situation at home.

I had been hiding newspapers since the strike had started and Da had been doing his bit by turning the radio down or the television off whenever the news came on. But as things worsened on the picket line, it was no longer possible to hide the truth from Mam – the whole street was talking about it. She was naturally devastated that her only daughter was all over the press, for what seemed to be all the wrong reasons.

'Why is it only your name they're saying, Mary?' she kept asking. 'Mary Manning this, Mary Manning that – what about the others, where are they? Are they gone back to work?'

I felt powerless to control what had started here and as I barely understood the situation in layman's terms myself, it was becoming more and more stressful to explain it to Ma. Increasingly, I found myself retreating to my bedroom in order to avoid the confrontation. To make the situation worse, Ben Dunne and Dunnes Stores management were refusing to negotiate our return to work on any level.

Disliked by some and adored by others, Ben Dunne was, and still is, a flamboyant and colourful character who polarises people in both his business and personal life. To understand the extent of the wealth, power and control Ben Dunne exerted in Ireland in 1984, it's important to understand that he ran not only the biggest low-cost supermarket chain in the country, he ran the only one. Essentially, he had no competition at this end of the market. Born into one of the wealthiest families in Ireland Ben Dunne was the son of a self-made multimillionaire. His father, Ben Dunne Snr, had opened his first shop in Cork in 1944 and by the time of his death from a heart attack in 1983 he had built his empire to over seventy outlets. Upon his death, the business was turned over to all six of his children and, while most of them played an active role in the company's operations, the actual leadership of the company became the responsibility of his youngest son, Ben Dunne Jnr.

Ben Dunne Jnr photographed in his office soon after he became director of the Dunnes Stores chain. The picture on the wall is of his late father, Ben Dunne Snr (© Derek Speirs).

Having inherited the top job along with a fortune, Ben Dunne was now one of the wealthiest men in the country and with that came huge economic clout – something he was not afraid to use. The 1980s were also an era of increased privatisation, pro-capitalism and the concept that profit came before people, creating a society that turned a blind eye to this behaviour. By the time the strike started, I had never met him face to face but knew enough people who had had dealings with him to know what we were up against. Notoriously short-tempered in his business dealings, when it came to any kind of negotiation there quite simply was none: it was the Ben Dunne way or no way. As we marched in circles outside his shop on Henry Street, hoping for the situation to be resolved, this was the attitude we were facing.

Each day that melted away now slowly revealed the reality that our union had been wrong – very wrong. One letter after another arrived from other unions and companies that supplied Dunnes Stores, stating that while our action was a courageous one, it could not be supported for varying reasons – most of them were honest in admitting that the financial implications of going against Ben Dunne and his company were just too great, both for them and their workers.

Amongst these rejections of support was a letter that presented us with a huge and unforeseen setback – unforeseen because the organisation concerned had no financial dealings with, or economic reliance on Dunnes Stores. It was from a representative of the Garda union. 'I regret to inform you that the Garda are co-operating fully with Dunnes Stores, Dunnes Stores security and their workers in bringing all deliveries to the store.'

Not only were they stating that they could not lend us any support, they were also informing us categorically that it was Dunnes Stores they would be supporting. While initially it came as a huge shock, the overriding effect of this news was to wake us up to how ridiculously naïve we all were. From day one our relationship with the Gardaí had been very friendly. We were a group of young, mainly single, women and they were, for the most part, young men, so there was the inevitable banter and flirting as we all spent long hours on the picket line. I think because of this we just assumed that they would have our backs if things ever got difficult. But after the arrival of this letter the whole atmosphere changed between us. They became more bureaucratic in their attitude and we, in turn, were now suspicious. The laughs and light-hearted enquiries as to how our strike was going now turned into demands that we remain inside the legal perimeter of the picket area and that we must keep moving. We never knew if they were officially instructed to change their behaviour towards us; all we knew was that the change was sudden and came without warning. We were dealt yet another blow shortly after this, when it transpired that the Gardaí weren't the only institution opposing our action.

The dominant cultural institution of Irish society in 1984 was still the Catholic Church, whose public stance in relation to the wider world was the support of justice and equality. As our action was about a human rights issue and we were in desperate need of some form of support, a decision was taken to approach the well-known Bishop of Galway, Eamonn Casey. Casey was a hugely influential public figure and was also the chairman of Trócaire – an Irish Catholic charity set up specifically to overcome the challenges of poverty and injustice overseas. Casey was not only loved by the public but he had a huge power within political circles as well. To get support from someone who had a celebrity-like status in Ireland would be an instant boost, because it would mean instant support from multiple tiers. I remember waiting in anticipation for his response, hoping that this could be a true turning point for the strike. I envisioned the moment Casey realised we were being vilified for trying to help impoverished and persecuted people and most likely jump at the chance to defend us.

Astonishingly, it was from him that the most damning attack on us emerged. In a private letter to John Mitchell, Bishop Casey described our action as 'economically harmful to the already impoverished Black South Africans'. He then went on to call our request for support from the Catholic Church as 'impertinent' and said that we should have consulted him and Trócaire before entering into the strike. This response, although private, shattered our confidence to the core for we knew that if he went public with his stance it would surely finish us off. His hard-hitting words also left me in a greater quandary about whether we were doing the right thing. Here was a man who had worked on the missions, fought relentlessly for impoverished Irish immigrants in the UK and was seen by most as progressive in his thinking. His popularity remained undimmed until 1992, when the scandal in his personal life became public knowledge. Casey had fathered a son in 1974 with his young housekeeper, Annie Murphy. After failing to persuade her to give up the baby for adoption, he forced her to keep it a secret and used Church funds to support them. Ultimately these actions were the cause of his downfall but at this point, in 1984, Eamonn Casey was one of the most influential men in the country and his reaction left us with serious questions about our actions.

We contended with one blow after another during these first few weeks on the picket line but the truly disheartening attack came with an announcement from the Minister for Labour Ruairi Quinn on behalf of the government, stating 'that while they were fully committed to opposing the Apartheid regime the dispute was an industrial one and for that reason they could not intervene'.

Ruairi Quinn had become Minister for Labour after the general election the year before when a coalition government was formed between Fine Gael and Labour. He was the son of a grocer from an upper middle class family; well-educated and a good rugby player, he had attended St Michael's College and Blackrock College. Being a member of the Irish Anti-Apartheid Movement Ruairi Quinn would also have moved in the same circles as Kader Asmal, but in spite of this and also him being a member of the Labour party, which, by rights, should have represented the ordinary worker, we were quite shocked when he showed his cards very early on as a person not willing to intervene. Although it was by now widely known in government circles that Dunnes Stores and their management were completely refusing to engage in talks either directly or through the Labour Court, it was clear the government were washing their hands of this contentious situation.

Minister for Labour Ruairi Quinn (right). A long-standing supporter and sponsor of the Irish Anti-Apartheid Movement, he is pictured here attending a meeting to celebrate the seventy-fifth anniversary of the ANC in 1987. To his left is John Hume (© Derek Speirs).

It now seemed to us that there was no one in our corner: the Irish government had sided with the economic powerhouse of Dunnes Stores. As if to remind us directly that we had crossed swords with a very powerful adversary, a letter arrived from management informing us that if we didn't go back to work with immediate effect we were all dismissed.

In my short time on the picket line I had learnt, in an abrupt and brutal manner, a very unsettling lesson about the meaning of equality – and how little it signified when you are a 21-year-old working-class girl. Ireland was a country run by men – priests, politicians and businessmen – who wined and dined each other and carried out the real deals, not in the pulpit or the office, but at the bar or on the golf course. Who were we? Ten working class shopworkers, nine women and one man, in a recession-hit country, where most felt lucky even to have job, striking about an issue that affected people in a country thousands of miles away.

Stuck between a rock and a hard place, tensions became very strained amongst us as the reality of our situation finally hit home. We were out on strike about an issue we knew little about and we didn't even have the full support of our own union. On the other hand, if we returned to work now, we believed that Dunnes Stores would find a way to have us sacked within days. And who was going to hire a striker just sacked from their job? We had taken on something far bigger than ourselves and this realisation was terrifying.

Feelings of fear, isolation and regret were now dominating my everyday life, both at home and on the picket line. As if sensing the deepening crisis, our co-workers intensified their abuse, but now in far more personal way. Late one afternoon I was alone on the picket line, the others having gone to block a delivery out the back, when I heard a voice calling out my name from the canteen window above.

'Hey, Mary.'

I ignored it and kept walking, but now at a pace, as I knew that a downpour of food or beverages normally followed the abuse.

'Word on the street is you have a bit of a thing for black men,' another voice hollered.

A chorus of giggles followed, accompanied by an arsenal of wet teabags, one of which landed on my head. I said nothing and didn't look up. I removed the sodden teabag that was now trickling cold tea through my hair and down the sides of my face and then just kept walking, indignantly circling the perimeter of the picket line, trying to block out the noise. I wanted to walk away – from them, from Henry Street, from the godawful situation I had somehow got myself into. But instead I kept walking, round and round in circles, counting my footsteps as I walked, until the taunting and the laughter had receded and I knew they were gone. Then I then stopped, not caring if the gardaí came along to move me on. They could arrest me for all I cared. I let my placard fall to the ground and wiped the cold tea from my cheeks with my sleeve, but no sooner was it gone than drops of hot tears replaced it. In this moment, I reached rock bottom, and in my heart of hearts I really had no idea how much longer I was going to be able to carry on. I took a minute to myself, in the brief quiet, and sobbed. Despite having all the strikers close by, I felt completely alone in that moment and, if there was a higher power in this universe, I felt it had completely abandoned me.

5

The Freedom Fighter

Growing up, I had never been a great believer in fate. It was a vague concept, and in Catholic-dominated Ireland, it was always associated with religion. So, call it divine providence or cosmic intervention, fate was never prominent in my thoughts. This all changed the day a man by the name of Nimrod Sejake joined us on the picket line. Up till now, the Dunnes Stores strike had been a whirlwind of changes and turning points, but none were as crucial, integral or pivotal to our story as the arrival of Nimrod.

It was a few weeks into the strike and Tommy, Alma, myself and a few others were pacing the main entrance of Dunnes Stores with our placards in hand and our spirits dampened with the disappointments of the previous weeks. Although a few kind supporters from Labour Youth, particularly Kevin McLoughlin, had begun to join us on Saturdays, we otherwise had made no impact on the public. As we circled the shop front on one of the many days when it was just us strikers, I noticed a man walking towards us, dressed in a white shirt, long, grey trench coat and a flat cap. His clothes were well worn but this was not the reason he grabbed my attention. He was black – the first black person I had laid eyes on. It may be hard to believe now, but in 1980s Ireland the only black people living here were either the families of diplomats and ambassadors or a very lucky privileged few who could afford to travel here and study at the likes of Trinity College Dublin or University College Dublin. All these people would have moved in very different circles from us.

By the time this man reached us I realised he was quite elderly, mid-sixties maybe. His face was worn, etched with the signs of a hard-lived life but his eyes were kind and from the sides of his capped head I could see tight silver curls protruding. Quietly, in a soft, broken accent, he told us that he was a South African exile living in Ireland and asked if it would be possible for him to join our protest. We were a little stunned, even intimidated, perhaps by the unfamiliar or maybe because this was the first real support that had come our way since the dispute had begun – either way we had no objection and from that day on he arrived every morning at the picket line and did not leave until the last of us did.

Nimrod Sejake was a quiet and unassuming man and it took a while for us to get to know him but as we did the effect on each of us was profound. For his first days on the picket line he said very little, practically nothing, and I soon realised that he was a man who waited to be asked a question rather than just speak out. He had a naturally unobtrusive presence about him. But I remember word for word the response he made to a question from one of us about what his homeland was really like. He held up his right hand as though there were a glass in it and said, 'You have to imagine South Africa as a pint of Guinness – the vast majority of it is black and a tiny minority is white – and just like a freshly poured pint, the white sits firmly on top of the black.'

In two brief sentences Nimrod Sejake had drawn a clearer picture in my mind of the South African situation than anybody had since the start of the strike. It was one of those pivotal moments that never leaves you because the visual image left in your head is so lucid. I

Nimrod Sejake on the picket line outside Dunnes Stores on Henry Street in July 1985 (© Derek Speirs).

know that each one of us felt the same and as our connection with Nimrod deepened we found out more and more fascinating details about his life.

Born in 1920 in a small townland just south of Johannesburg, Nimrod was one of the lucky few to attend a mission school and he later went to the Wilberforce Nature College where he qualified as a teacher. He then worked at Mooki Memorial College in Johannesburg, but was sacked from his post in 1953 for refusing to teach under the newly implemented Bantu Education Act. Bantu Education was a carefully designed act, conceived by the apartheid government with a single aim in mind: to keep their unskilled labour market in abundant supply. Languages, maths and sciences were all banned and replaced with sewing, cleaning, farming and classes in other menial work, resulting in millions of black South African children being trained specifically for a life of slave labour. Appalled by this, Nimrod refocused his efforts on opposing the apartheid regime. A founding member of the South African Congress of Trade Unions (SACTU), he rapidly became a hugely influential labour and union organiser for South Africa's

Outside Dunnes (l–r): Nimrod Sejake, me, Tommy Davis, Alma Russell, Michelle Gavin, Liz Deasy, Sandra Griffin, Karen Gearon, Theresa Mooney and Cathryn O'Reilly. Nimrod, our mentor, always stayed in the background, away from the limelight (© Derek Speirs).

working classes. He joined the African National Congress (or ANC, the national liberation movement formed in South Africa in 1912) and quickly moved up the ranks to become an ANC leader in Soweto where he lived. All throughout the 1950s he was hugely involved in the increasingly radical defiance campaign of demonstrations against the apartheid regime and the organisation of workers' strikes. These activities led him to be arrested with 155 other members of the ANC accused of treason against the state. Nimrod shared a prison cell with Nelson Mandela during the infamous 1957 treason trials. Soon afterwards, he was forced to flee his country or face the death penalty, leaving behind his wife and four children. By the time he arrived on our picket line he had not seen his family for over twenty years.

Rarely in my life have I been in a situation where my particular outlook and views on something have so quickly and radically changed. Since the strike had started, I had come to view Henry Street, specifically the entrance to Dunnes Stores, as a place that brought on a sense of dread and fear. Each time I got off the bus and walked my usual route over the Ha'penny Bridge, it was as though dark clouds were gathering. The closer I got to the picket line the stronger the feeling became – the hostility and the resentment towards us left little to look forward to. But soon after Nimrod arrived, these feelings waned and replacing them were hope, eagerness and, despite our circumstances, optimism. Because the picket line was offering me something completely different, I now had a spring in my step – somehow Nimrod's voice, singular and authentic, was blocking out all the noise that had for weeks left us downcast.

When Nimrod spoke about his country it was in lyrical terms, with unbridled passion and muted pain. He described South Africa as a beautiful land, richly endowed with wonderful resources, a place where there was more than enough for everyone. But the white minority, only 20 per cent of the population, had seized 87 per cent of the land. This left black people trapped in poverty-stricken townships, ghettos of misery filled with cheap and often slave labour, whose sole existence was to maintain this hugely wealthy white minority. Nimrod rarely spoke about himself on a personal level but when he did it was in the form of an illuminating tale, for this is what Nimrod was: a storyteller.

We learnt that in 1950 a law was passed by the new apartheid government where South African people had to be racially classified as white, coloured, Asian or black – a compulsory test that Nimrod himself had undergone. The most infamous of these was the 'pencil test', which said that if a pencil placed in a person's hair fell out, he or she was white. If it fell out with shaking, the classification was coloured or Asian and if it stayed put, the person was 'black'. They put a pencil through Nimrod's hair and it became stuck. They looked at the moons of his fingernails and saw more mauve than white, which indicated black blood. It was decided there and then that he could not own land, he could not vote and he could not leave his home without a pass. Nimrod was classified as black, which, under apartheid law, automatically deemed him a person of inferior race, a substandard being. Nimrod was not a man looking for sympathy or veneration. He wanted only to illuminate for the world the atrocities suffered in his country that had been shrouded in darkness for too long. As a teacher, his firm belief was that education was the key to bring about change – irrespective of class or colour. We were now his pupils and our classroom was the grimy chewing-gum-spattered pavement at the entrance to the shop we were all on strike from. Spending time with Nimrod was expanding our minds and forcing us all to view the world through an entirely different lens.

My journeys on the No. 78 bus to and from work were no longer anxiety filled, driven by a fear of what lay waiting for me at either end. The lone poster on my wall of Bruce Springsteen was now accompanied by a new hero: Nelson Mandela. Time spent alone in my bedroom became periods of reflection when I tried to absorb fully all that I was hearing. Random and abstract information, little echoes of learning from my schooldays, which had seemed irrelevant at the time, now began occupying my thoughts. Before this I could never correlate abstract learning with something real, something tangible, but now my consciousness was swirling with recovered data, trinkets of information and different quotes.

'All animals are equal, but some animals are more equal than others.'

The more I heard from Nimrod the more this line from George Orwell's *Animal Farm* came to the forefront of my mind. To me, this was apartheid, a system that promoted inequality that was defined by one thing only: the colour of a person's skin. At first it was hard for us on the picket line to believe that such a regime existed. It seemed almost implausible that a country could have over 80 per cent of its population, upwards of 20 million civilians, living in such inhumane circumstances. But even more difficult for us to comprehend, once we'd learned about the regime, was that every Western government was still doing business with South Africa. They were, in effect, supporting a regime that had no higher regard for the life of a black

South African than the Nazis had had for the life of a Jew. And this is where Nimrod was able to explain to us what others could not, for as a black South African he had lived it from the day he was born.

The apartheid regime exploited the black South Africans, using them as slave labour to build and maintain their booming economy. So, with Western governments turning a blind eye, apartheid and global economic growth worked in tandem. He explained that black South African workers were the first link in a long economic chain. The benefits for them were nil, but each link in the chain after this was a lucrative one – one where everybody, to varying degrees, was a beneficiary. The farmers, the shippers, the distributors, the governments around the world, the banks, the retailers, the wholesalers, the marketeers and the traders were all profiting from the fruits of slave labour. The last link in this intricate chain was us – shopworkers on the tills of a supermarket on Henry Street in Dublin, the capital city of one of the smallest countries in the world. Although only ill-treated and lowly paid shopworkers ourselves, it did not take long for us to grasp that, as part of this chain, we were as accountable as the next person. Each time we registered the sale of a piece of South African fruit or vegetable we were condemning its people to a life of misery. We might have been working class, we may have been uneducated, but we knew the difference between right and wrong.

Our political enlightenment did not happen overnight; the learning involved was a gradual process. Yet the shift in our mindset was swift and unambiguous and this was down to Nimrod. His motivation for change and his passion for equality couldn't have been more authentic or transparent, not just for black South Africans but for us as workers. Here was a black man who had witnessed and helped mobilise the emergence of the black workers' resistance movement against the abhorrent apartheid regime and he was telling us that our actions were what the black South African community had been calling for all along.

We, as a group of people, now fully comprehended the importance of the pivotal moment those two Outspan grapefruits were pushed to one side of the till where we worked. This naïve action had, in effect, weakened one small link in a booming economic chain. But even now, weeks into our strike, it was still an insignificant crack, hardly visible at all because it had been made by the most unlikely people, a group of working-class shopworkers. We now understood that it was our responsibility to force that small fracture into a number of gaping holes that would grow impossible for those in power to ignore.

The atmosphere on the picket line was rapidly changing. The days, which had once felt like weeks, now flew by as we immersed ourselves fully into this learning process. Hair, makeup, clothes and boy crushes were off the agenda, paled by the significance of our new focus. We no longer waited like lost souls for the latest update from our union or bothered to engage in pointless spats with our abusive colleagues. We just didn't have time: there was too much to discover that was so much more meaningful.

Now that we had a real focus and a common purpose we began to unite in a way I would never thought possible before Nimrod's timely arrival on the picket line. By giving us the much-needed confidence that what we were doing was helping the South African cause he had armoured us with a sense of conviction. Most crucially we were all now agreed on one primary issue: our action was no longer about a union directive or our rights as workers. We now had a clear focus on what we were doing and, most importantly, why we were doing it. Thousands of miles apart, the first and last links in the chain now stood together in solidarity. As long as we were required to handle the sale of South African goods we would never return to work in Dunnes Stores. We had learnt too much from Nimrod about the atrocities in South Africa and there was no turning back. From this point on we were no longer following a union instruction; we were following our hearts. We, the Dunnes Stores Strikers, would remain on the picket line for as long as it took until we had the right, as workers and as human beings, to refuse to handle this tainted produce.

6

Building a Movement

Soon after Nimrod arrived on the picket line, a minor tension became obvious, which struck me as somewhat strange. It was only a minute thing and I would have forgotten it quickly had a few other strikers not noticed it too.

I had imagined that Nimrod and Kader Asmal, being fellow countrymen who suffered under the same horrific regime, would have naturally been drawn together. But this was not the case. There was an indifference between them, which, although restrained and unspoken, was obvious, and on the occasions when Kader appeared on the picket line, Nimrod seemed to sink into the background. Here were two people endeavouring to highlight the same issues, occupying the same space, our picket line, but who appeared to have nothing whatsoever in common. It didn't play too much on my mind at this stage because we were benefiting greatly, in different ways, from the support of both men. Kader materialised on the picket line on Saturdays, with a much-needed surge of energy and dynamism. His commanding speeches, which seamlessly flowed together with provocative points and emotive words, won over the small group of journalists and supporters that gathered. In the hour or two he graced us with, Kader shone a brighter light on our action than we, ten shopworkers, could do in a week of walking around in circles on the picket line. His presence, while fleeting, was central to our action and the survival of it. In contrast, Nimrod's presence, although a quiet, unassuming one, was constant and steady. Nimrod provided us with was something that Kader Asmal's busy schedule would never have allowed for. He had time to educate us, the time to give us the tools we required to start building a real movement, our own movement.

Our first group meeting to start building a movement began more like hen fight than a strategy offensive – a bunch of babbling fools all talking over one another. There was quite simply no time to listen because everyone had so much to say. I'm eternally grateful that Dunnes Stores management never got to witness us in those moments as they would have laughed at our total failure to communicate with each other on any level. Finally, it was Brendan Archbold who casually pointed out that it might be an idea if we actually listened to each other. While at first some of us took offence to his coolly made criticism, we all understood the point he was making. And so we learned the invaluable lesson to listen, not to speak over each other and to let everyone have their say.

As we considered ways of moving forward we looked to Nimrod. He had told us about Martin Luther King Jr and how his efforts in the 1950s and 1960s to end racial discrimination and segregation in the US had offered a beacon of hope to all striving for freedom in South Africa. It seemed to me that Nimrod often relayed specific stories to empower us for a particular situation. He told us about other women who had in the past stood up for change and equal rights for all – for example, Rosa Parks, an African American, whose simple act of refusing to give up her seat on a bus to a white man in 1955 had helped initiate the whole Civil Rights movement in the United States. These descriptions of how great change has only ever been achieved by the empowerment of the bottom levels of society made us feel like we could do the same. He explained that Martin Luther King Jr, in trying to achieve his greater goal of racial equality, plotted out a series of smaller objectives that involved local grass-roots campaigns. Ultimately, it was the importance of this type of grass-roots action that became ingrained deep into our psyche as we learnt that, if properly respected and utilised, it had the potential to alter an entire way of thinking.

We were now understanding that we, the strikers, were the grass roots, the bottom of the political pyramid, the opposite of the Establishment who had so aggressively pitted themselves against us, for reasons that were becoming increasingly obvious to me. If you were already rich and powerful, why would you want to disrupt the normal flow of things? The suppressing of any desire for change was imperative to maintain the status quo and this was the reason why we, and anybody who supported us, were put under duress. I also now understood how branding us as troublemakers and radicals was to create a fear in people about our action. The same had happened in South Africa with anybody who opposed the apartheid regime: they were branded Communists and linked to Russia at the height of the Cold War when the Western world had a deep-rooted fear of that political system. We, like them, needed to be isolated from the most likely place that support and empathy would come – the general public. We all now knew that to move forward, we, as a group, had to set about making our own strategies to spread the word.

Looking back now, I believe the reason we came together with such ease is that we were only a small group. Maybe if there was a larger number of strikers it would have led to schisms within the group, but because there was so few of us it was easier to stick together. We couldn't afford to splinter because it would have made continuing the strike impossible. We were thrown together because of the strike; some of us wouldn't really have known each other beforehand: Theresa and Vonnie worked in the cash office, Tommy and Liz were part-time and worked evenings, only starting at 5 p.m.

when most of us would have been nearly finished. We got to know each other for the first time on the picket line, but we were now sticking together because of it. We had our arguments and differences of opinion but we decided very early on that this could not spill out into the public arena. What happened behind closed doors had to stay behind closed doors – otherwise we could not survive. We were a small enough group to be able to discuss everything and all decisions we made were on a majority-rules basis.

Soon, we all slipped into different roles on the picket line. Karen and Cathryn were both excellent and natural speakers and soon became the people most interviewed by the media. I would be interviewed too as my name was the one mainly associated with the strike, but it did not come naturally to me and in the beginning my knees would be shaking and my palms sweating. But no matter who was interviewed and received media attention, no one person was more important than the others or the strike, and if for a second they thought they were, they were quickly put in their place. Alma was the joker but she was fearless and passionate. Theresa, Sandra and Michelle may have been the quiet ones but with this came a dogged determination. Vonnie was the more mature one while Liz, as the youngest, was not hindered in any way by her age. And Tommy, the only man amongst all us women, was as determined and resolute as any of us. He also had an abundance of patience to put up with the lot of us. Between the ten of us there was no weak link.

We spent hours writing up pamphlets setting out our goals, to try and explain the reasons why we were on strike and then handed them out to passers-by and shoppers. We began to invite who we considered like-minded people to stand with us on the picket line, including the Labour Youth, Sinn Féin, Afri (Action From Ireland) and other more left-wing organisations. This worked on one level, because each of these organisations brought with them new supporters, but it also presented us with our first big dilemma.

Each political party and organisation that supported us now asked us to join them in return. If it had not been for Nimrod I am sure we would have jumped at this but he had forewarned about the implications that could arise from this – linking ourselves directly to anybody else's policies would leave us open to criticism. For example, if we joined Sinn Féin we could be accused of supporting the IRA, if we joined Labour Youth we could become embroiled in discussions on their broader political policies, all of which would distract from our very singular action against apartheid.

After lengthy discussions, we, the strikers, made our first important collective decision – a pact not to join any parties or organisations for the duration of the strike. This was a chicken-and-egg situation, where we recognised the importance of gathering support but in turn couldn't risk alienating anyone, particularly the public. In doing so we risked losing all the support we had recently gained. But our risk paid off and I think it made people realise that we had evolved into a very serious group who were making well-thought-out decisions. In a matter of days, we could see a small swelling in support beginning to build. Members of Labour Youth, Independent TDs, the anti-apartheid movement and trade union members were now regulars on the picket line. We also began to hear murmurings of support coming from Leinster House from higher-ranking Labour TDs such as Michael D. Higgins and Brendan Ryan, and Independent TDs such as Tony Gregory and Joe Higgins.

All the while the atmosphere on the picket line was changing in the best way possible. I could visibly see support around us growing and I knew that if it was visible to us out on the picket line it must also be to Ben Dunne and his management inside the shop. The divide was deepening; the Establishment on one side, us, the strikers, on the other, two sections of society hugely opposed to each other's methods and ways of thinking. With this came a mounting feeling of restlessness as we all waited for Ben Dunne and his management's next move. Little did we know, their next plan was under way and, like all their other actions against us, the ultimate aim was to completely undermine our movement. It all came to light one evening when Cathryn O'Reilly, who had just come off duty at the delivery entrance, came around the front and asked, 'Has anybody else noticed there are far fewer trucks arriving than there was last week?'

She was right: the traffic in and out of the delivery area of Dunnes Stores had eased off considerably. Things had been quieter for about a week, maybe even more. Rapid discussion escalated on the picket line as we tried to figure out what was going on. I began to wonder if Ben Dunne had privately come under pressure from the government to stock South African goods no longer, or perhaps was encouraged to make some effort to phase out the goods. We wondered had we been too much hassle for him, had we somehow, unbeknownst to ourselves, finally made some impact. We knew Ben Dunne would never publicly back down, not to people like us, but perhaps privately he was backing off and hoping it would all just go away.

I peered through the windows. From where I stood I could see a huge yellow mountain of South African Outspan grapefruits staring back at me. That put paid to the notion that he was secretly phasing out the goods. What I couldn't fathom was, if they weren't being delivered through the back entrance and they weren't getting in the front entrance, how was the produce getting into the shop? A few of us decided to wander around to the Moore Street Market to see if any of the marketeers, many of whom had become our friends, had noticed anything. It didn't take long for us to find out what was really going on. Despite our political enlightenment, this day proved that we were still not immune to moments of huge naivety.

Ben Dunne's resourcefulness in ensuring his Henry Street store remained stocked up with South African goods surprised even us. While we were sound asleep in our beds he had the deliveries arriving under the cloak of night in unmarked vans. We were shocked and slightly humiliated that he had us caught us napping but this was a game changer, one which convinced us to make an immediate decision: to bring a halt to this situation we would have to start picketing through the night.

That very night we began a through-the-night campaign that was to result in a wholly unexpected predicament for us: a new level of harassment and intimidation towards us from the Garda Síochána. When the unmarked trucks arrived so did the gardaí. You always remember the fights you lose, and we certainly lost that night. Up until now the gardaí didn't really bother us. Yes, we endured the occasional pushing and shoving during delivery times and telling-off when not moving on the picket line, but it was nothing sinister. However, that night outside the delivery entrance, things took a disturbing turn, one that would change our relationship with them for the rest of the strike.

There were about three gardaí to every one striker, a true show of brute force. But in my naivety, I really believed that if things were going to come to a head the protectors of society would not let us get harmed. As the trucks pulled in, we stood at the delivery entrance, linked arm in arm. The delivery men tried to push the crates straight through us but when we knocked the crates out of the way the gardaí made their move.

They charged at us in force. Two gardaí went for Alma and she clung to the delivery door, determined. But Alma had recently got engaged and her ring ripped against her finger. She let out a cry of pain as she was hauled away by two large men. None of us could help her, as we had all been descended on. Two officers cornered Cathryn, and while she cowered against the back wall of Dunnes Stores, one of them hissed at her that the ring on his finger was made from good South African gold made by her 'nigger friends'.

They continued to intimidate and divide us, all the while phrases like 'nigger lovers', 'look after your own' and 'you should be thankful for a job' were hurled abusively at us. We were forced to watch helplessly while the deliveries were made, in the knowledge that we had seriously underestimated how far the Irish police force would go to ensure the normal flow of operations continued and that physical force against women would be used if necessary.

That night all of us returned home battered and bruised but something far more pivotal had happened. We might have been physically broken by the actions of the gardaí but mentally we, as a group, were as strong, if not stronger, than ever. Rather than take this lying down, as they had probably hoped we would, we decided we couldn't just ignore what happened.

We made a complaint to the gardaí about what had taken place in the darkened alleyway at the back of Dunnes Stores. Unsurprisingly, this got us nowhere. When it became clear that no one from the force was going to own up to or point the finger at what had really happened that night, we decided it was time to take a different route. In a time when there were no mobile phones, no Internet, no Facebook or Twitter, the one source of information everyone had was the press – and it was to them we needed to highlight what was happening. From that night on, each time we could see things about to escalate on the picket line, either I or one of the other strikers would run to the battered phone box across the street and call the press.

While Dunnes Stores and the Establishment were trying to keep things quiet, we were making as much noise as possible. Very soon, small sections of the media were no longer portraying us as the scourge of society, but rather as the victims in an increasingly murky David-and-Goliath tale. We had by now been on strike for several months and while our impact was as yet a minor one, we felt we were making progress and finally moving in the right direction. Most days on the picket line it was still just us along with Nimrod, who walked the three miles from his Red Cross hostel in Ballsbridge to Henry Street each morning and back again each evening. But come Saturday it was an altogether different story – often up to 200 people would join us on the picket line. Increasing numbers of media would arrive and often up to four of us were being interviewed simultaneously. Having support lifted our morale on the picket line, in spite of all those who opposed us. I felt especially proud on the Saturdays, where you could visibly see the support growing, and I was glad on the Saturdays that Kader Asmal would turn up because it felt as though we were proving that the media attention he'd invested in us was worth it.

As if to cement his belief in us and what we were doing, Kader

Asmal invited all the Dunnes Stores Strikers to attend the Annual General Meeting of the Irish Anti-Apartheid Movement at the end of September 1984. I remember leaving my house that evening feeling unusually nervous. The picket line was my home now and I didn't relish the idea of being pushed out of my comfort zone into the unknown territory of the AGM. But this event turned out to be one of the most memorable things that happened to me throughout the strike – a night that left me in the knowledge I still had much to learn about South Africa and apartheid.

Marius Schoon, a white South African and anti-apartheid activist, was there to tell his harrowing story, one that he hoped would help the wider world understand exactly how far the South African government was willing to go in order to maintain their regime. We quickly learned that Marius Schoon was a rare breed in South Africa, a well-educated white man, who from an early age had campaigned and fought for equal rights for the black majority in his country. Any opposition to the apartheid government was considered to be a serious crime and soon he was arrested. He was reprieved from the death penalty, which he openly admitted was probably due to the colour of his skin, but was sentenced to twelve years in prison where he suffered horrific treatment at the hands of the South African police who abhorred the disloyalty he had shown.

Soon after his release he fell in love with Jeanette Curtis. However, they were banned from seeing each other for their anti-regime activity and were not legally allowed to communicate, so they fled South Africa and sought refuge in neighbouring Botswana. The Schoons were warned that they were still targets of the apartheid regime. By now they had two young children so they moved to Angola where they felt it would be safer for their family. Marius was out of town when Jeannette, watched by their six-year-old daughter Katryn, opened the letter bomb meant for him. A palpable and heartbreaking silence gripped us all as he then described how he had flown home as quickly as possible, to find his wife and daughter splattered across the walls of their flat. His three-year-old son, who had witnessed the whole thing, was found wandering in the street alone outside the crime scene. In one cruel moment, apartheid forces had destroyed this man and his family's entire life. And what compounded the moment further for me was the knowledge that this had all taken place just four months beforehand on 28 June 1984.

(L–r): Cathryn O'Reilly, me, David Kitson and Marius Schoon pictured at the AGM of the Irish Anti-Apartheid Movement in September 1984. David Kitson, like Marius, was white South African who opposed the apartheid regime; he had served twenty years in a South African jail for his activities against the state (© Derek Speirs).

At the end of his talk I fought back tears as this incredible man took my hand in his and thanked me and all of us for our strike action. Here was a man who had lost his wife and child fighting the apartheid regime and he was thanking us. Our sacrifice was nothing compared to his. Ultimately, this was further proof, as if we needed any more, that we were doing what black South Africa wanted us to do – this man had lost his family doing it. I was completely humbled by the whole experience and was felt grateful to Kader Asmal for giving us this opportunity to hear Marius speak.

That night I got the bus home alone. Staring out of the grime-stained windows onto the darkened streets of Dublin, the yellow beams from street lamps flicked past my eyes. I thought about Marius Schoon. His words and his story had moved me deeply and it would be a memory I would carry with me forever. In spite of everything, Marius Schoon was still resisting, still fighting and still publicly shaming his own white South African supremacist government for its horrific, unacceptable regime. Most would have buckled at such personal loss, crawled under a rock and let someone else take up the mantle, but not him. Marius Schoon was a man made more determined by their actions against him – a man who would not be silenced.

As I drew closer to home I began to think about Mam, something I had been doing quite a lot of lately. An unstated truce had evolved between us where we never spoke about the strike. It was as if it wasn't happening at all. She would greet me in the evening with, 'How are you, Mary? How was your day?'

I would reply with some innocuous detail about my day – any detail would suffice, as long as I didn't mention the dreaded strike. This had suited me for a while but in recent weeks all this phoney conversation had begun to agitate me, mainly because her behaviour made no sense. She had brought me up to know the difference between right and wrong, to defend the weaker or less fortunate in society. These were not just beliefs she had implanted in her children, they were also ones that she put into practice in her own daily life. When a traveller family moved into our area Mam was the first person on our street to invite the mother into her home. This woman became a regular visitor – and Mam didn't care what anybody thought of that. I also remember distinctly her calling me out over an incident that happened when I was six years old. I arrived home from school one day and told her that everybody was saying that the new girl was smelly and that we shouldn't sit beside her or we'd all start smelling too. Mam was outraged. It was moments like these that she instilled into me the necessity to be always mindful of those who were not as lucky as we were – and asked who were we to know or judge anything about their lives. This was why my agitation with Mam was beginning to boil over to the point where I wondered how much longer I could suppress it. It was all such a contradiction – she was a contradiction.

Mam had always called me wilful, which was a bit ironic because if there was ever a reason for me being wilful it was her. She had inspired a great sense of self-belief into me since I could remember. Now, the very person who had imparted this drive to me, to live my life by the simple rule of knowing right from wrong, was inexplicably denying her support when I needed it most. I knew her fears were rooted in where all of this might lead for her daughter into the future, and that they were genuine concerns, but increasingly I felt it was not a good enough reason for her to have such a negative reaction towards me.

As I got into bed and snuggled up to my beloved Patch, Mam called to me through the partition wall (it was so thin that she could have whispered and I would have heard her).

'How did your day go, Mary?'

I had to bite my tongue. I so badly wanted to tell her about the AGM, about Marius Schoon and his harrowing story – and mostly I wanted to tell her the simultaneous joy and sorrow I felt when he thanked me for what I was doing. But I couldn't. I took a deep breath and supressed the urge to let all this pour out and instead I whispered back:

'It was all good, Mam.'

We both knew it wasn't. I didn't know when, but sooner or later this charade between us was going to implode – I think even Da and the boys could feel it. But little did I know as I drifted off into a deep, exhausted sleep, a situation was to occur on the picket line the very next morning that would force me to examine my mother's attitude towards me.

7

When a Stranger Calls

The picket line was now a scene where gossip and rumour flowed freely, which could sometimes create an atmosphere of paranoia and suspicion. Apart from our union updates, our daily lives had become a guessing game as to what would occur next and who would be responsible. One rumour, which had been going around for a while now, was difficult to believe. Apparently, priests around Dublin were telling their parishioners from the pulpit at Sunday Masses not to support our strike. Although Bishop Eamonn Casey had sent his damning stance on the strike in a private letter to our union, the Church had remained silent, so in many ways this rumour just didn't seem plausible to me. Why would priests, many of whom had been missionaries in South Africa, openly condemn our action against this horrific system? They would have either witnessed first-hand or at the very least possessed a far deeper knowledge about the apartheid system than most ordinary Irish people, so it didn't make any sense that they would oppose us.

Of course, I should have learned by now to assume nothing! A shocking twist occurred, proving that very little made sense when it came to the stance of the Irish Establishment regarding our action – especially those who had power and knew how to use it. We were standing on the picket line the morning after Marius Schoon's talk, all still high from the previous evening's poignant events, when I noticed a couple of elderly nuns walking up Henry Street, carrying wicker shopping baskets. My initial reaction was disbelief: they could not possibly be about to do this. As they approached us, I realised that yes, they were here to defiantly pass our picket.

In spite of my Mam being deeply religious I had never had much time for or interest in the Catholic Church. She was under the assumption that I attended Mass every Sunday – I didn't. I would generally leave the house and just go for a walk. I was born into a generation who were on the cusp of the huge split from the Catholic Church and while all the damning and haunting revelations of abuse had yet to be exposed, I think that a good deal of us suspected that there was something intrinsically wrong with the institution of the Catholic Church.

As the nuns came closer, we, the strikers, drew together to block the entrance. We started with our usual banter about the reasons for striking and offered them our handmade leaflets that could further educate them on why our action was necessary. All of this fell on deaf ears but when one of the nuns began to explain to us that our action was harmful to black South Africans we knew at once their action was not a singular one. The very words that Bishop Eamonn Casey had written in his letter, condemning our action as 'impertinent' and 'economically harmful to the already impoverished Black South Africans' were spilling from her mouth. In that moment, any notion that I had had regarding reports of priests damning us from the pulpit as being mere rumour or salacious gossip evaporated. What was happening here needed no discussion or dialogue between us strikers – we all knew very well that this was a message from the top and these elderly nuns had been sent to preach it to us directly.

It was Cathryn O'Reilly who reacted the most strongly. The rest of us stood back and watched her with awe and admiration as she singlehandedly took on these nuns. We all felt that, for Cathryn, this was not just about the strike. Cathryn was a single mother, with a beautiful son, Jonathan, and, although this was less than four decades ago, the grip of the Church on the Irish psyche and our consequential behaviour was still vice-like, particularly in their heartless attitude to young unmarried woman and their children.

Just six months before our strike had started, Ann Lovett, a fifteen-year-old schoolgirl from Granard, County Longford, and her baby son died, completely alone, after she had secretly given birth to him beside a grotto dedicated to the Virgin Mary. Despite her being full term, not one member of this tiny community admitted to knowing she was pregnant. The shutters of silence slammed down and to this day what really happened to Ann Lovett and her baby has never been confirmed. Only three months later, in April 1984, the infamous Kerry Babies case came to light: two newborn infants were found at different locations in the same town, one brutally murdered and the other abandoned at birth. The deaths of both infants, while separate, were the result of a community's desire to cover up any shame these births could bring to them. But which was the greater shame: the fact that babies had been born out of wedlock or the failure of society that led to the deaths of these innocent newborns and a young girl? It may be difficult to understand today, but by 1984, the decades of control and fear exerted by the Catholic Church left the Irish population resorting to silence and evasion as their only coping mechanism.

Cathryn O'Reilly was a single mother who lived at home with her parents. The last mother-and-baby homes shut only in the early 1990s, so the notion that this treatment of young mothers happened long in the past is simply untrue. With pride, Cathryn, quite rightly, showed Jonathan off for the world to see, so that morning when the nuns arrived on our picket line with the sole aim of shaming us and our action, Cathryn, of all people, was not about to take their vitriolic attitude lying down. Once it was made clear that the nuns had no interest in listening to the reasons for our action, by eventually describing it as disgrace to the Irish people, all hell broke loose. Inhibitions put aside, Cathryn retaliated robustly by questioning their morals, their total lack of empathy and their ignorance as to the suffering of black South Africans.

I had admired Cathryn greatly from the start of the strike. She was hugely articulate and a force to be reckoned with but that morning when I saw her take on the heartless, petty messengers of the Church, even shouting after them once they had crossed the picket and entered the shop, I realised that, in many ways, she was braver than

Cathyrn O'Reilly remonstrates with a nun who came to the picket line to preach to us about the harm we were doing to the black South African people (© Derek Speirs).

the rest of us. With a responsibility to her young son, then barely three years old, she had more on her plate and much more at stake than any of us. She never reneged on her picket-line duties and on days when she had no one to mind Jonathan, she simply brought him with her.

Once it was over and the nuns were gone, we all rallied around Cathryn. The anger that she just vented was probably one that had built over the months, or even the years. However, it quickly dispersed and was replaced by a different emotion. She was completely shaken and close to tears – but these were not tears of self-pity or defeatism; they were ones of conviction. Cathryn O'Reilly had proved to us and to herself she was not willing to stay silent in the face of any adversity, no matter where it came from.

That evening, as I walked from the picket line, I decided not to go directly home. The last two days had been exhilarating but emotionally exhausting. They had also caused an unexplained shift within myself, which had sparked, in many ways unwanted, internal questioning about Mam and her own view on the strike. I walked over the Ha'penny Bridge towards the south of the city and meandered through the streets until I found myself sitting alone on a wooden bench in St Stephen's Green, needing time alone to think. As the evening sun dipped in the sky I threw the remnants of a half-eaten sandwich from my lunchbox into the pond and watched a paddling of ducks battle furiously long after the last crumbs were gone.

I have never been a person to make impulsive decisions – when faced with a quandary or moment of doubt, it's just not in my nature. I need time alone to reflect, weigh things up and figure everything out within my own mind before I can reach a decision or, hopefully, find an answer. While for most of my life I have found this helpful, and it usually means my decisions are concrete, it has also on occasion made me slow to recognise a situation brewing under the surface, until it's about to boil over. This was one of those occasions. I now reflected on my own deeply personal reasons for resenting both the state and the Church and their appalling treatment of women and children, and that's when the penny dropped. The reasons for Mam's reaction to my part in the strike suddenly dawned on me. I couldn't believe it had taken me so long to realise this, given what I knew of her personal history. It was not the strike that Mam feared, it was not the outcome of it and nor was it what other people thought of her or me: it was the Establishment she feared, for it was these structures that had shaped her as a child into the adult she was now.

*   *   *

It had all started decades before, with my maternal grandmother's unplanned pregnancy. On 23 March 1930, she gave birth to my mother in the Coombe Hospital in Dublin. For much of my childhood, I knew none of this. I have no idea when Mam planned to tell me the truth or if she ever planned to at all, but when a stranger called to our door, this was probably the moment Mam realised she could not keep things under wraps forever.

I was eight years old and home alone with Mam when the doorbell rang.

'Will ya get that, Mary?' she hollered from the back garden where she was hanging the washing out on the line.

I opened the front door and saw a lady standing there. She was older than Mam but not that much. Two things immediately struck me about this woman. The first was that she was beautifully dressed in a woollen suit, fur coat and jewellery. Nobody on our street dressed like this and jewellery was for extremely special occasions. The second thing was that I had never set eyes on this woman before. Kilmainham was a small area, where everybody knew everybody and we rarely, if ever, had strangers calling at our door. For a moment she said nothing, then asked, 'Is your mother home?'

I called in to Mam, who by now was making her way to the door. I could tell from Mam's face that they knew each other so when she told me to go off down the road and play I ran down our narrow pathway as fast as my little legs could take me, excited to see my friends. It was a busy and adventurous afternoon and by the time I returned, the woman was gone. Although I noticed that Mam and Da spent an unusually long time that evening alone, deep in conversation in the kitchen, I didn't really think about it again.

A few months later Mam asked me if I remembered the woman who had called to the door. I said that I did. Who could forget a fur coat like that? Mam seemed very pleased about this. She then told me that this lady was in fact my Auntie Mollie and that we would be going to meet her for a walk. The next day we went and met my new Aunt Mollie at the Royal Hospital Kilmainham, which was very close to where we lived. At that time the old hospital building, which had served as a retirement home for soldiers, had been derelict for over forty years and fallen into complete disrepair, but, despite being completely overgrown, the grounds were used by all the Kilmainham locals. Over the following few years Mam and I would go and meet Mollie, not regularly, but every few months. More often than not we would meet in Dublin but on a couple of occasions we took the train down to Mallow in County Cork where Mollie lived, and stayed at her house. Her husband had passed away and, never having had any children, she lived alone. Mollie seemed very close to her older sister Bridget, who lived a few doors up from her, and when we were there I would play with her grandchildren. My brothers, Lar and Brian, never met Mollie and I never asked why because I just presumed that they, being older than me, had better things to be doing with their time. Although I could never say I was very close to Mollie I really grew to enjoy the time we spent with her. She bought me clothes and toys we could never have afforded in our house and I guess what cemented my fondness for her was the very obvious affection my Mam had for her.

Fast-forward to two years later. I am ten years old and sitting at our kitchen table, peeling the potatoes with Mam for our dinner. Da was at work and the boys were out. I had always been an inquisitive child and I know that both Mam and Da were often driven mad by my persistent questioning of everything. However, in fairness to Mam, no matter how bizarre or how far off the wall my curious mind ventured, she always had an answer to everything. Today was no different. I had a new question for her, one that had been on my mind and prompted by something my first cousin Ann had told me the previous week.

'Why does Ann say we're not really first cousins?'

Mam stopped peeling the potatoes almost at once and, in that split second, I saw an anxiety in her face that I had never seen before. For a while she did nothing but then stood up and, with her back to me, began washing the dishes. At this moment, I understood that Mam might not have an answer for this question or, if she did, it might not be as straightforward as I would have wished for.

My ten-year-old mind was beginning to reel but just as I was reaching the point of panic the strangest thing happened. Mam turned around and I could see that all anxiety had disappeared from her face. She sat down beside me and said, gently, that I was right: Ann wasn't my first cousin and that Ann's mother, Margaret, was not her sister. Until that very moment I had genuinely believed that Mam had a sister, Margaret, and two brothers, Tom and Jack. I thought that they were my aunt and uncles, that their mother was my Mam's mother, and my grandmother.

Before I could decipher all this unexpected news and ask another question, Mam went on to explain that she had been born out of wedlock and had gone to live with her adopted family in Swords, who were distant relatives. She then assured me that although she had never met her mother or father she had been very lucky in her life and had always been made to feel very happy. Mam made it all sound so normal that I just accepted this story as fact. I was ten years old so why would it even occur to me that Mam, although thrown by my question, had a prepared answer for it long before I had asked it?

Time went by and as I grew older so did my inquisitive mind and, by the time I reached adolescence, I began to suspect that Mam's story of her childhood didn't quite add up. I noticed intricacies about Mam that might well have always been present, but that I had been too young to absorb. I would catch her in a deep moment of silent sadness and although I could not be certain, I felt it was all connected to her

Mam, back left, with her 'Swords family', in the early 1940s.

earlier life. I was by now a busy fourteen-year-old so this was not something that dominated my thoughts but, in moments alone with Mam, I would occasionally probe or ask the odd difficult question in an effort to get to the bottom of things.

'So if your "Swords family" are distantly related, would they not know who your Mam and Da are?'

In these moments, Mam shut down. With the deftness of a person who had much experience of it, she would swiftly change the subject and I would know that that was the end of that – until one day when, without warning, everything shifted dramatically. To this day, I have no clue what motivated this turnaround for Mam; all I know is that I didn't have to ask her one question. The truth came pouring out – well, some of it anyway.

Auntie Mollie was her birth mother and the first time Mam had met her was the day she called to our front door. Until that day Mam didn't know her own mother's name, had never heard from her before and had no idea she would turn up that day. Although I had long suspected that Mam was carrying more secrets and this completely threw me, what Mam told me next broke my heart. The moment she laid eyes on Mollie standing at our front door she knew instinctively that this was her mother. I remembered how I had assumed, mainly by Mam's reaction, that Mollie was not a stranger to her. I asked Mam if Da knew all of this and she assured me that he did. Lar and Brian did not, but she had told Da before they married. I found it a bit weird that the boys, being older than me, only knew about the 'Swords family', but the relief that Da knew was enough for me.

Now some more devastating truths were revealed. Mam had not lived with her 'Swords family' from birth. Mam had started her days at St Vincent's industrial school in Goldenbridge, a state-funded residence run by the Sisters of Mercy to take care of orphaned children or those like Mam who were born out of wedlock. During these years she would sometimes be fostered by different families around Dublin, moving frequently, and had only been taken in by the 'Swords family' when she was eleven years old. At the age of thirteen she was then placed into service as a housemaid for a family of solicitors called the Brennans, whom I knew because Mam still cleaned for them. She did go back to stay with her 'Swords family' at weekends sometimes but in reality she had only ever lived with them for two years of her life.

Mam must have seen the complete horror rising in my face and was very quick to reassure me that she had been very lucky and that, despite everything, her childhood was a very happy one. This I took as fact because I had no real reason to doubt she was telling me the truth. I also had another far more pressing question to ask her. If Mollie was her Mam, and in turn my grandmother, then why, when we were with her, did we call her Aunt Mollie? This is when Mam became awkward. Looking back, I think she hoped I wouldn't ask this question, for the answer was far more painful than finding out my Mam had spent the first ten years of her life with no permanent home.

Apart from Mollie's older sister Bridget, whom I had met the few times when we had gone to Mollie's house in Mallow, and Mollie's mother, who was by now long dead, Mam's very existence was a shameful secret. Mollie had seven other siblings who had no idea she had secretly given birth to and given up a daughter in 1930, nor did any of Mollie's friends or extended family know about Mam.

Mam seemed happy enough to accept that things must stay this way. In fact, her greatest concern of all was that nobody else, apart from me and Da, know the truth about Mollie being her Mam, including both of my brothers. None of this sat easily with me and Mam knew it. I just couldn't fathom why she was so accepting of Mollie's wishes that she, her daughter, remain a secret – a shameful secret. But, of course, the bottom line was that Mam was just extremely grateful her mother had sought her out after all these years. And while it was not exactly the relationship she would have wished for, it was clearly the best she was going to get. So, in spite of my deep-rooted belief that her gratefulness and acceptance about her situation with Mollie defied logic, ultimately it was something I could understand. Mam had found something she had yearned for her entire life and, for the sake of her desire to cling to what she had found, I agreed with her wish that her secret remain just that: a secret.

Reflecting back now and being privy to the true inner working of the Irish Catholic Church at that time and the decades preceding it, I realise now that my fifteen-year-old self had become just another pawn. Here we were, three generations of women from the same family – a grandmother, mother and daughter born over fifty years apart – all intimidated into going along with their horrific game of silence and secrecy.

That day I had been left with far more questions, most of which Mam could not, or perhaps would not, give me answers to. Did she ever live with Mollie or was she given up on the day she was born? Did she know who her dad was? Mam, being Mam, would always manage to turn my inquisitiveness into something positive. She would delight in repeatedly telling me that Mollie had named her Josephine before she gave her up. She also told me that Mollie had refused to sign her over for adoption like so many other unmarried mothers had done with their children. There were occasions, prompted by my frustration at my Mam's insistence on viewing life through rose-tinted glasses, where I would be sorely tempted to point out the irony of things she was telling me, such as the fact that Mollie had named Mam Josephine but that Mam was completely forbidden to address Mollie as who she really was – her mother. But I never did because no matter now exasperated I became I knew deep down that Mam didn't deserve to hear this. Titbits of information would be given, little details of happy moments, that would steer any conversation away from the bigger questions and perhaps more painful answers.

By the time I found out all of this I had not seen my 'Aunt Mollie' in a while but after Mam told me the truth about Mollie I never laid eyes on her again. Although Mam never said it, I don't think that she felt she could trust me not to say anything that might rock the boat or might make Mollie disappear out of her life again. Mam would leave the house in a flurry of excitement when she was going to meet Mollie in the Gresham Hotel, where she stayed whenever she came to Dublin, and on these days I felt very happy for her. Mam had somehow managed to turn a very difficult situation, which could so easily have become crippling, into something very positive in her life. But the truth was that Mam was in a fragile bubble, one that was unfortunately going to burst less than three years later.

I don't know how long I had been sitting on that wooden bench in

St Stephen's Green when the park attendant tapped my shoulder and informed me he was locking up. Forced out of my reverie, I saw that the sun was long gone and that the light was rapidly disappearing from the evening sky. As I gathered my things and made my way out of the park I thought back on all that had happened over the previous couple of days. I realised now that meeting Marius Schoon, a man who refused to be silenced, combined with witnessing Cathryn's refusal to bow down, had, in many ways, forced me to view Mam's attitude towards the strike from her point of view. I was now blessed with a far greater understanding of the fear she was experiencing and with this came huge empathy towards her.

Marius Schoon had been brought up in a privileged environment. He was highly educated, well off and had been given all the building blocks as a child that help to create a strong inner core, ones that could not be easily dismantled in later life. Cathryn, although not born into money, had been blessed with other necessities that helped mould her into the woman she became, mainly a family that offered unconditional love and support when she needed it most. Mam had no such infrastructures – she had endured a childhood filled with uncertainty, secrecy and rejection that began the moment she was born. She had never been given proper love, care or support in her formative years and as a result she buckled under pressure. In fact, the life she found with my father was a true achievement for a person who had such a precarious start. The very moment my mother had been conceived in her mother's young womb, her future was already decided by the Church and the State – one that destined her for a life of rejection, abandonment and denial of her own existence. Along with that, the very people who had choreographed all these painful hardships then required her to keep the details of them hidden as shameful secrets that could eat someone from the inside out. Her whole childhood had been an intense tutorial on keeping silent or facing the consequences. Unlike Marius Schoon or Cathryn O'Reilly she had quite simply been given no capacity to stand up against the Establishment.

I jumped off the bus and walked up the narrow pathway towards my house with a rage burning inside me towards the Establishment who had made Mam like this. I turned the key in my front door but before I pushed it open I took a deep breath and then another in an effort to calm myself down. The Dunnes Stores strike had been going for just over two months now and during this time I had already gone through huge internal and personal change, which was gradually allowing me to view the world from a very different perspective. Mam could never know this, for it could possibly break her, but the strike was no longer just about black South Africans, it was now also for her and what she had suffered at the hands of the people who were now pitting themselves against myself and my colleagues.

They might have given Mam a childhood that left her mute with fear in the face of adversity, but she in turn had gifted me with something entirely different: an ability and strength to speak out without fear of repercussion. That night before I went to sleep I went into Mam's bedroom and for the first time in months I sat on her bed and we chatted about everything and nothing, just like the old days. But in my mind the battle lines were already being redrawn – this had just become personal.

8

The Many Faces of Power

The seasons were quickly changing and, as the sunny months of July and August made way for cool September, a rather dismal October slowly crept upon us. The days of sunbathing at the back of the building were but a blissful memory and Karen no longer needed to patrol for anyone catching a few rays. However, the concrete slabs of Henry Street's pavement, which we marched with determination, were still where our tutelage began each morning.

Support was increasing slowly, both at home and abroad, and with each new person who refused to cross our picket line and instead stood by our side, our confidence grew. Each day that passed brought new learning, new ideas and the working-out of intricate plans that could highlight our cause and hinder any further sabotage attempts from those against us. In fact, we became so preoccupied trying to foresee what our next battle with Ben Dunne and his management might be, we weren't watching our backs or worrying about the people we already had support from. Just over three months into our action, we were given a critical lesson in how the upper echelons of society and those with influence really worked, from Kader Asmal.

It was this blow that completely knocked us as it was so unpredicted and unexpected. I had noticed since our attendance at the AGM of the Irish Anti-Apartheid Movement the previous month that we had seen Kader only once or possibly twice on our picket line. I didn't pay much heed to this because firstly, he was a busy man, but secondly, we had all become so media-savvy that any interviews about the strike were now mainly carried out by us. Because of the very public acknowledgement and respect he had shown at the AGM, I had no reason to suspect that there was anything amiss in his relationship with us. But once again, we were about to be completely wrong-footed.

In late October Kader Asmal asked for a meeting with John Mitchell and Brendan Archbold at the union head office. The meeting began with Kader promptly informing them both that the strike had gone on long enough, that our point had been made and that it was now time for us to go back to work. When Brendan came to tell us, we stood there, placards in hand, wind blowing violently through our hair and a look of shock and betrayal etched across all of our faces as we attempted to absorb the news Brendan was giving us. Kader Asmal, the head of the Irish Anti-Apartheid Movement, was pulling his support from our anti-apartheid strike – the very man who had demanded a boycott from the Irish public. By any standards this seemed like a loss of epic proportions to the strike – and we all knew it.

Brendan could see the impact this news was having on us and was quick to point out that he and John had not conceded to this ridiculous request. Instead they had asked Kader his reasoning. Apparently Kader didn't have much further to say on the matter other than that he felt our strike had gone far enough and he did not want his withdrawal of support to cause any embarrassment by spilling out on to the streets.

It came as a huge relief that both Brendan and John remained adamant in their support for us and we even managed to have a laugh at Brendan's comical description of Kader trying to cut and run from the meeting only to be stopped by John, who only allowed him to leave after he had made it clear to Kader that the strike would not end until there was a satisfactory resolution for us strikers, one with dignity. But what Brendan said next struck us all as very odd: Kader had told them he would not make his feelings on our action public – he would keep them to himself. The hardest thing for us to digest was that Kader Asmal and the IAAM had been asking for a ban on South African goods – here we were, taking the action of a boycott, only to find ourselves rejected by the very organisation that was asking for it.

The rest of that day proved to be a difficult one as we all wondered where this news was going to leave us. While Kader said he would not publicly go against us, how could we trust him now? We were also

On the picket line (l–r): me, Tommy Davis and Karen Gearon. Seán McBride is in the background (© Derek Speirs).

acutely aware of the very powerful circles he moved in and if he was willing to disparage us privately, it was unlikely that his personal feelings about our action would remain a secret, particularly from those who would be relieved to hear that he had pulled his support. Later that day as I trudged along the picket line I remembered back to when I had first noticed the indifference between Kader and Nimrod so I asked Nimrod where he thought all of this would leave us.

Without pausing for even a moment of reflection, Nimrod assured me that nothing whatsoever would change. He explained that Kader had nothing to gain by going public with his change of heart and that, in fact, the fallout from any vocal opposition to our strike could have a damning effect on both him and his organisation. And in that moment the realisation hit me: of course he would do or say nothing. Like Bishop Eamonn Casey, who only months beforehand had done the same thing, Kader was hoping by privately voicing his opposition to our action to bring an end to the strike. But this was not something he would take a risk on publicly. The fact was that these were both men whose lives were a balancing act. They were walking the fine line of trying to retain public opinion while ensuring not to rock the boat for themselves within the upper tiers of Irish society, in which they enjoyed equal popularity. In order to maintain this, their lives became a multifaceted high-wire act, where a different face was required depending on who they were dealing with. The benefits that Kader enjoyed from his strong public opinion and from moving in such powerful circles almost guaranteed his silence. I now asked Nimrod another question: why had Kader Asmal done this to us?

'Kader Asmal wants action, just not your type of action.'

Nimrod's short reply was an all-encompassing one, and one that needed no further explanation for me. Ultimately, what really separated us, the Dunnes Stores Strikers, from Kader Asmal was how we viewed the change process. Kader was an influential, well-respected and educated man who firmly held the belief that change could only come from the top down. And why not? He ran among the highest intellectual and political circles in the country where everything was discuss first, act later. But this was completely at odds with what we had learnt from Nimrod, and now firmly believed ourselves, that people power was the only real driver of change. Kader's thinking was entirely at odds with the whole movement we had started, a grass-roots movement. This movement was not led by affluent men, well-educated lecturers or powerful politicians, the type of groups Kader would have wanted to endorse the strike; instead it was led by us, a predominantly female group of working-class citizens, supported largely by the general working-class public, left-wing politicians and a South African freedom fighter. What made our movement so inspiring to some were the exact same reasons that caused embarrassment for Kader Asmal.

That evening after Dunnes had closed, I stood outside the shop for a while chatting to some of the other strikers. In the distance, I could see Nimrod walking away down Henry Street. His movements were slow and jaded and it was clear that this was pure exhaustion after another long day on our picket line. As he turned the corner and disappeared down O'Connell Street to begin the three-mile trek home to his hostel I felt nothing but compassion for this man who had been through so much in his sixty-three years and who, like a force of nature, was still fighting the struggle with every ounce of passion in his body and mind.

All that had happened today had further deepened my respect for this amazing man. The difference between Nimrod and Kader was all too clear now. Here we had two South Africans, both treated cruelly by their home country, both viewed as less important and having fewer rights than the white minority and yet, because of their different positions in society, their different positions on the class tier, one black, one coloured, they had completely different views on how to achieve their goals successfully. We were naturally drawn to Nimrod because, like him, we were working class, but for that very same reason we never really clicked with Kader. While I believe he respected the idea of a boycott, I am not sure that he respected *our* boycott.

If Kader's rejection had happened earlier in the strike, before Nimrod had arrived, the effects of him abandoning us would have been detrimental – in fact, it would have been surprising if the strike had lasted any more than a few days. But as I said goodbye to my co-strikers and strode away from the picket line I knew that we all felt the same: yes, we had been dealt another blow but we had now learned to roll with the punches and pick ourselves up far quicker than before. While we were shaken by Kader's attempt to call off the strike, we still had the most supportive South African voice we could wish for: Nimrod's. Nimrod, who persevered through the long hours, late evenings and bitter weather conditions each day, side by side with us, not just an ally, but a friend. And on the days we needed it most, like

Addressing an IAAM march: beside me is Cathryn O'Reilly holding her son, Jonathan (© Derek Speirs).

the day just gone, he was always there for us – a steady, reliable and reassuring hand that guided us through rougher waters.

It was hard to know what Kader had hoped to gain from pulling his support 'privately' but there was one thing that was becoming increasingly obvious: in spite of his personal feelings about our strike there was a very large group within the IAAM who continued to support us. Looking back now, I believe this could have been another troubling factor for Kader – our strike was splitting the IAAM in two. There were those who came to the picket line to support our action and then there were those who went to wine-and-cheese parties to support the IAAM. He could not see a way of making the two factions in the movement work together. Many of the leading sponsors of the Irish Anti-Apartheid Movement in 1984, including Labour Minister Ruairi Quinn, had been happy when the problem was far away but the strike action had brought it to the fore, politically and economically, and it was all becoming too close to home for them. What Kader and all these people failed to understand was that this was no longer about us, or our rights as workers, but about those who couldn't go out on strike like us, or publicly condemn apartheid like him – this was about working-class black South Africans. Circumstances had also changed since Kader first met us, and so had we, individually and as a closely knit group. And the fact remained, the few hundred or so who turned up religiously every Saturday to swell the picket line were not doing it for Kader or any organisation – they were doing it because they, like us, had a deep-rooted desire to bring an end to the abhorrent apartheid regime.

9

Small Cog in a Big Wheel

One of the earliest memories I have of my Da was when I was in senior infants at school. We were learning how to knit, so I decided to make him a tie in a canary-yellow wool. I vividly remember the Friday he arrived home from work and I presented him with my weeks of hard labour. Back then Da was still in the army, and the vision of a soldier walking around our neighbourhood wearing a bright-yellow knitted tie was greeted with deafening howls of laughter from the rest of the family. Da loved all of his children equally, but, being his youngest and only girl, I had from a very young age found ways of getting my Da, a quiet and reserved man, to do things he would normally not. So in spite of Mam, Lar and Brian's insistence that Da wouldn't be seen dead wearing the tie outside the house, the very next morning with my hand in his, he walked me to our local shop to spend my five pence pocket money. I was very small, but I still remember looking up that bright yellow tie around his neck with the feeling that this man would do anything for me. It is a feeling that never once left me while Da was alive.

As the strike became tougher, the days became darker and money got tighter, Da became my steadfast support and a huge comfort to arrive home to each evening after a long day on the picket. He was never too vocal in front of Mam but when I needed advice he would listen carefully, discuss with interest and try to help me find solutions to the many obstacles we faced on a daily basis. Mam was still very uneasy with regard to the strike but, in fairness to her, she was supporting me in other ways, by always checking that I had eaten enough or that I was wearing the right clothes, buying me clothes and throwing me a few bob. Brian and Lar did their bit too. Recognising my constant struggle to live on the strike pay of £21 a week, they would often stuff a few quid into my hand.

Back on the picket line, our recovery from the Kader Asmal debacle was swift. It was only a matter of a day or two before we had refocused our minds back on to what really mattered. Kader pulling his support was not something that we would have wished for, but in many ways we had been taught a vital lesson – to watch our backs at all times, for it was never going to be clear where the next renegation of support might come from, or what might motivate it. Kader's wife, Louise, a lovely soft-spoken lady, still visited the picket, but we rarely saw Kader himself again. We had to move forward and hanging around pondering over what he had done and why he had done it was only going to hinder that.

Before October was out, our supporters decided to throw a Halloween party, and it was such moments of good-natured fun and friendship that made it possible for us to keep going. The mucking-around between us on the picket line in the days leading up to the party reached fever pitch as we each tried to guess what the others would dress up as. I told everyone I was going as either Ben Dunne or Bishop Eamonn Casey but I actually had other plans under way! During a break from picketing I had run over to Frawley's Fabrics on Thomas Street to buy some material for my outfit – a rare luxury I was going to allow myself. That evening I went home and began work on what proved to be a far more elaborate undertaking than I had envisaged. Three nights later, I was still working on it and at this stage I had managed to rope Mam in. It's not that she had wanted to help me, she just couldn't bear to watch the ongoing tussle between me and all the materials I had gathered to complete my outfit. Eventually, after many stops, starts and a few exasperated desertions of my idea, I figured out a way. I got five wire clothes hangers and opened them out to make one big circle and then two smaller circles. Mam had an old thin foam cot mattress so I sewed this around all three circles, placing the large one in the middle and the smaller ones top and bottom. At this stage, Mam, Da and the boys were falling about laughing but I felt some pride now that I could see my outfit taking the desired shape of a huge hollow foam ball. Everything had taken so long that I was still sewing the material I had purchased from Frawleys on to the giant ball an hour before the party was due to begin. Once I stepped inside the ball Mam cut two holes it for my arms and then we glued on the blue sticker I had made the night before: 'Product of South Africa – Do Not Touch.' On the other side was a label that said 'Danger: Contaminated With Apartheid'.

Ten minutes later I was on the No. 78 bus on my way into town dressed as a giant Outspan grapefruit. I had somehow struggled on to the bus at the stop outside our house but at the other end I had to be helped off by two other passengers and the bus conductor, all in convulsions. I then waddled up Dublin's main thoroughfare, O'Connell Street, passing countless shoppers and commuters who must have thought I was deranged. When I reached Parnell Square where the party was being held I bumped into Brendan Archbold who had come dressed as a priest. It took nearly five minutes for us to catch our breath to even say hello to each other. That Halloween was one I will never forget, and for many reasons other than our insane costumes and the craic that was had. We, the strikers, as a group of people had already bonded but now something else was happening that I had not really witnessed before. We had a core group of supporters for our action at this stage who were, for the most part, working class but from all walks of life, including students, teachers, postal workers, nurses, office

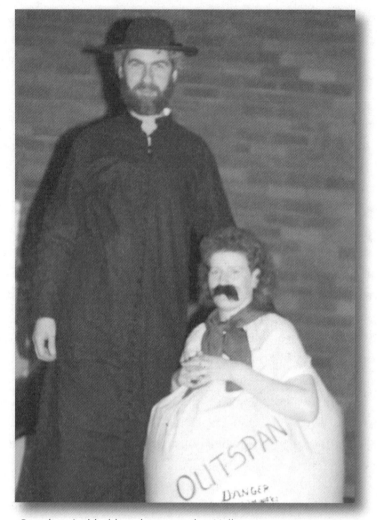

Brendan Archbold and me at the Halloween party in 1984. Dressed up as an Outspan grapefruit, I am wearing a moustache given to me by one of the other party goers!

workers on their lunch breaks and even shopworkers from other department stores. They would come and go from the picket line but increasingly more and more faces became regulars and, from this, our action felt sturdier and somehow more resilient to outside forces that wanted to bring it to an end. Other successes were happening too. With this increasing support from people who were now personally invested in our action came help, the kind we badly needed.

Word was filtering back to us through Brendan that John Mitchell was having growing difficulty maintaining the support of his executive. They were putting him under pressure to bring about a quick resolution, even threatening that there was only so long they could continue with our strike pay. But in Ben Dunne, John Mitchell was dealing with a man who was not only refusing to negotiate our return to work on any level, he had ordered his management to follow suit. Then there was the Irish government: Minister for Labour Ruairi Quinn was happy to issue letter after letter advising us that this should be taken to the Labour Court, but how could this happen if the government was not willing to take proper action and force Ben Dunne's hand. Many TDs had been members of the IAAM years before the strike started and we expected them to support us or at least try to intervene because of the moral implications of selling South African produce. The fact remained that the longer the strike went on, the worse the financial strain on us, the strikers, would become.

This is where the much-needed help from our supporters came in: a strike fund was started and soon we were attending small events and gigs around the city that had been arranged by our supporters, all proceeds from which went into the fund. While it was not loads of money it left us secure in the knowledge that if our union carried out their threat to halt our strike pay we had something to fall back on. These fund-raising events also served the dual purpose of us being able to rally even further support.

But as it always appeared to be with our strike, even in our moments of success, another obstacle was never far from sight. The increasing numbers on the picket line heightened tensions between us and the gardaí. There were times they even confiscated the buckets of money that we had collected from our fund-raising effort – no receipts would be given, our protests would be laughed at and we never saw the money again. Looking back I have often wondered how these burly men, armed with batons, really felt taking on a small group of mainly young women, some of us as young as their own daughters. Did they ever, in a quiet moment away from the picket line, discuss with each other how odd it was that they were expected to do this? Did they ever question who they were really 'protecting and serving'? It would be comforting to think at least a few of them had moments of doubt, but the next two incidents that happened gave little evidence that any one of them allowed such thoughts to venture into their minds.

Our strike was beginning to make waves across the water and Arthur Scargill, the leader of the miners' strike in Great Britain, which had been going on for over nine months, decided to come to Ireland to meet us. The meeting was to take place at the Mansion House in Dublin, so, late that afternoon most of us left the picket line early while a few stayed to finish the day off. Tommy Davis was one of them. During a late delivery out the back of Dunnes Stores, he and a few others blocked the entrance in an effort to stop it and, while doing so, Tommy knocked a carton of eggs to the ground. Tensions rose quickly, as they always did, but this time the garda reaction was dramatically different from anything we had experienced before. The moment the eggs fell to the ground, a Black Maria van pulled up right beside Tommy and two gardaí exited the vehicle.

Without a second's warning, they dragged Tommy by the scruff of the neck and the last sight anybody caught of him was his face slammed into the van door and his smashed glasses falling to the ground. The remaining strikers followed the rest of us to the Mansion House and told us what had happened. None of us knew where Tommy had been taken or what was happening to him – but we could all take a fairly good guess and worried for our gentle, unassuming and kind friend.

When Tommy was released, he came straight to the Mansion House, determined not to miss meeting Arthur Scargill. He arrived there with his shirt ripped and his glasses broken. He had a cut over his eye and marks on his arms. He told us the gardaí had ridiculed him for being a 'nigger lover', a 'wimp' and an 'embarrassment of a man'.

Two gardaí outside Dunnes Stores on Henry Street. We often found the garda presence there intimidating (© Derek Speirs).

Tommy was the only man on strike and in my mind this made him more the braver for taking a stand with us. They probably did to him what they would have liked to do to the rest of us, but harming women was probably a step too far, even by the standards they had shown so far. And as is so often the case in Ireland, the 'bigger' man won – Tommy's claims of physical assault and intimidation by the gardaí were greeted with incredulity and probably worsened the case against him. He was charged with breach of the peace, incitement to violence and use of foul and abusive language. When brought to court all charges, except the one of use of foul and abusive language, were dropped, but he was bound over to keep the peace for two years – which meant essentially, if he had another run-in with the police he'd go straight to prison. All of this over a carton of eggs. If we needed any proof that the gardaí were above the law they vowed to uphold, this was it.

The next incident was the one that made us realise the gravity of what we had taken on. A new tactic was to move the battleground away from the picket line to the homes of the strikers, with visits from the Special Branch, a unit set up by the government, tasked with dealing with threats to the state. First it was Cathryn O'Reilly who arrived to the picket line one morning and told us that the previous evening a member of the Special Branch had called to her house. He didn't ask to go in and was casual enough, saying he wasn't there on official business and that he just wanted a chat. He asked her a few questions about the strike, why she was doing it, when it might end, and then left. The visit was brief and on the surface inoffensive but she was shaken up, leaving us all to wonder where this was leading.

Next it was Theresa Mooney. The following Saturday morning she opened her front door to a man who showed his ID as a Special Branch officer. He asked if he could come in for a chat but she refused. He then asked if she was the one who had first refused to handle the South African goods. At this stage Theresa felt that things were not right. Why would a Special Branch officer be sent out to ask questions like this? Now terrified, she said that she had to go out, that she needed to go into town. The officer offered her a lift, saying they could continue their chat in his car. Again she refused, and this is when things turned sinister: he said she was nothing but a small cog in a big wheel and to go back to work because she could never win. He added that he would be back again soon and, with that, he left.

This was the point we realised that some kind of action had to be taken. The following Monday, John Mitchell and Brendan Archbold stepped in, bypassing the Garda Síochána, who were clearly going to be of no help to us, and wrote directly to Minister for Justice Michael Noonan. We knew by now that nobody within the Garda Síochána could bring the behaviour of certain members under control, but maybe the man at the top could.

The letter to Michael Noonan was sent off with a mixture of hope and fear. We had become far more resilient to any adversity that we encountered but it was hard not to forget how naivety had tripped us up in the past. Ultimately, I suppose the hope and fear we all felt arose from us previously underestimating men with power. We were all so personally invested in the movement now that we wouldn't let them stifle our voices but, even as we grew more determined, it was hard not to worry that their tactics to try and silence us might become even more sinister.

10

The Parting Gift

Silence, enforced by suppression, is a truly powerful and effective tool when those in power seek to maintain control. Many months beforehand, Nimrod had taught us this through reference to South Africa, and since the strike had begun we had experienced at first hand these suppression tactics on a weekly basis at the picket line. Although we fought hard against it, and for the most part felt unbreakable, it sometimes hit our core, either individually or as a group. We were all shaken by the Special Branch officers' use of intimidation tactics towards two of our colleagues, in particular Theresa Mooney. Gentler and more sensitive than the likes of myself, Cathryn and Karen, Theresa had been a soft target.

I rarely, if ever, mentioned anything about the strike in front of Mam these days, but the day a letter from Minister for Justice Michael Noonan arrived back I stormed home to tell Da. The minister had tasked the gardaí with an investigation into our complaint and the letter contained the findings of that investigation. It stated that they found no evidence that any harassment or intimidation of the strikers had taken place whatsoever. As Da had been in the army for nearly twenty years, I wanted his opinion. Usually I had the sense to wait until Mam was out of the kitchen but this evening I was so animated, I didn't. Da was outraged but for the rest of the evening, Mam made it her business to warn me about the consequences of the strike and my actions. What did we expect if we went around rubbing everyone up the wrong way? Would it be our door they'd call to next?

By now, I understood the triggers that prompted Mam's fear surrounding the strike and her fear of challenging the Establishment, but occasionally, no matter how hard I tried to remind myself of her precarious start in life, Mam could get under my skin. Tension was rising between us and it was becoming difficult to hold back the anger and thoughts that were rushing through my mind. I eventually announced I was going out for a walk – it was either that or a massive row.

There was still some light in the day as I walked towards the Royal Hospital Kilmainham. As I strolled around the grounds admiring this magnificent building, recently restored to its former glory, I began to reflect fondly on the walks Mam, Da, Lar, Brian and I would have here most weekends when I was younger. Da would tease us with stories about dead soldiers and regularly terrify us into believing that one of their ghosts had just walked through him. As I walked further into the grounds I saw the tree we all used to climb and remembered the old swing – a tyre on a rope – that used to hang from one of the tree's strongest branches. Brian, Lar and I would all fight for a turn on it. As I walked towards the old tree, my legs began to feel the strain of the day's picket-line marching. I took a seat beneath the tree and in that moment, another heavier memory forced its way to the forefront of my mind. It was here, in this spot, that I had met 'Aunt Mollie', properly, for the first time. Without any sibling competition that day, I'd had the swing to myself, and as I went back and forth, higher and higher, I watched Mam and Mollie chatting below me on the grass, not knowing then that they were, in fact, mother and daughter.

As far back as I could remember, there were always people in and out of our house. Da was a quiet man who kept to himself but Mam was a natural socialiser and loved having 'the women' around. On those days, the table would be set and she would be in the kitchen cooking all day. If you opened the door to the sitting room on one of these nights, you would be greeted by a cloud of cigarette smoke and howls of laughter. As I stared over at the spot where Mam and Mollie had once sat deep in conversation I now recalled the day that all this conviviality in our home was brought to a sudden halt.

I had just turned seventeen and arrived home from school to find Mam crying inconsolably at the kitchen table. In all my life I had never seen her so distressed and it took quite some time before she was calm enough to tell me why.

Mollie had passed away – her mother was dead. Mam had read her death notice in the newspaper that morning.

As close as I was to Mam, I realised that I couldn't handle this situation on my own, and phoned Da to explain that he needed to come home immediately. If anybody could bring Mam around it would be him. But twenty minutes later he was standing in the kitchen looking, if anything, more worried than me. His efforts to console Mam made no further progress than my own had. Mam appeared slightly manic, telling us she had to go shopping for a new coat to wear to the funeral. She asked Da if he would drive her into town. We didn't say anything but by the look Da gave me I knew we were thinking the same thing. Mam was going nowhere near Mollie's funeral, never mind into town shopping for a new coat.

It was nearly six o'clock in the evening and it was only a matter of minutes before Brian and Lar returned home from work. I began to panic. How were we going to explain Mam to them? She was completely hysterical about her mother who had just died, and they didn't even know about Mollie's existence. Da and I didn't need to bother leaving the kitchen to speak about it, as Mam's state left her completely oblivious to what was going on around her. It was clear that this situation could no longer be kept a secret, and the boys needed to know about Mollie. After some discussion, I offered to tell them.

It was odd and unsettling as the youngest of the family to have to sit your two older brothers down and disclose a family secret you have known for years. A small part of me resented Mam and Mollie for putting me in this position, but I also felt some relief that we, as a family, were finally getting everything out in the open. Until that moment I hadn't recognised the weight this secrecy had placed on me. As the truth came pouring out, about Mollie, Mam and their relationship, a horribly uncomfortable atmosphere descended upon our living room. For the first time, Lar and Brian were discovering the existence of a maternal grandmother, one they had never met, a secret relationship between her and Mam that had gone on for nearly a decade, but in the same moment they were being told that this woman had died the day before. All these distressing details had to be absorbed while the sobs of their hysterical mother reverberated through the walls of the house.

As shocking as this information overload was, it was just a minor detail in comparison to Mam's traumatised reaction to her mother's death. I had gone to school that morning, waved off by a mother who, despite everything she had experienced, always tended to take a cheerful view on life, and arrived home to someone barely recognisable as the person I knew and loved. We were all totally unnerved but hoped she would get better from here. Little did we know that Mam's downward spiral had only just begun.

The next day Mam was worse. Da stayed home from work and I didn't go to school. Mam was even more determined to go to her mother's funeral than the day before and she now had a reason other than paying her respects. Mam wanted to have Mollie's wedding band. It was tradition that after a family death that the mother's wedding band was always passed on to the eldest daughter. This was true, and a point hard to argue with, as Mam was not only the eldest daughter, but Mollie's only child.

It seemed everything we were saying in an effort to stop her was pointless. If no one would bring her to Mallow, she would take train. At this stage Da and I were in despair. As far as we were both aware the only person in Mallow who knew of Mam's existence was Mollie's older sister Bridget, and we couldn't imagine the unannounced arrival of Mollie's secret daughter could play out well for Mam – and that's all we cared about. By the end of that day we were exhausted with her, and when she began to tell us that she also wanted the fur coat that Mollie always wore we realised that we needed help. We called her 'Swords family' over to try and talk sense to her. Mam still considered them her family and we regularly spent time with them. In recent years Mam had become very close to her 'brother's' wife, Phyllis.

Once Jack and Phyllis arrived, some desperately needed calm descended on the Manning household. We left Mam and Phyllis alone in the kitchen, hopeful that Mam could now be persuaded. But this was not the case. Phyllis tried her best but Mam was going and that was it. Phyllis offered to bring her and, realising that we had no option but to let Mam do what she felt was necessary, Da and I conceded to her wishes – on one condition made by me: that I went with her. I just couldn't bear the thought of Mam having to face her mother's funeral without me by her side, not under these circumstances. But Mam, suddenly rational for the first time since Mollie's death, refused. She said I was too young and I had to stay at home to mind Da and the boys. She was lying and we both knew it. For the same reason that I had never been invited to meet Mollie after I learnt the truth about her, Mam stopped me from attending Mollie's funeral – she didn't trust me to keep silent.

The next morning, we were all up early. Mam was still fragile, a jumble of nerves and worries, but she remained determined, if quiet. She had suffered a lifetime of denial and her mother's funeral was not another deprivation she was going to suffer. I stood on the footpath, watching the car pull away, and waved as she disappeared into the distance. For the first time I allowed myself to cry – hot, angry, hurt-filled tears – not for Mollie but for my Mam's broken heart and the brave soul that was now journeying into unknown and possibly hostile territory. I just hoped that she would walk away from all of this relatively unscathed. I even held a small hope that she would receive some form some of peace or closure. Alas, it was not logical thinking that was ruling my mind that day but naivety and blind hope.

I was not there to witness what had happened but by the time Phyllis and Mam arrived back to the house late that night, we could tell immediately from their demeanours that it had been a disaster. Mam was in a dishevelled, nonsensical state. Phyllis had had the foresight to bring some Valium and had, I think, given Mam some on the journey home. I undressed Mam and put her straight to bed. I then went downstairs and sat uncomfortably at the kitchen table with Da, Brian and Lar as Phyllis relayed the harrowing events of the day.

When Mam and Phyllis arrived in Mallow, they went straight to the funeral home, which was busy with mourners. It became quickly obvious that there was one person unimpressed with Mam's appearance: Mollie's older sister Bridget. While her greeting was not overtly hostile, it was cold and unwelcoming. Although a little unsteady after this frosty reception, Mam kept herself together until it was time to join the rest of the mourners to say a final decade of the rosary over Mollie's open coffin. At this point, Mam, unable to contain her emotions, began openly weeping. Once the prayers were finished and the coffin was closed over, Mam's status at her mother's funeral was made abundantly clear to her. Bridget asked to speak to them alone.

Without an ounce of empathy, Bridget explained to Mam that her presence was inappropriate and suggested that she go back to Dublin at once. I would have thought that the person who I had seen leaving our house that morning, my Mam, would have been crushed by this but she stood her ground and told Bridget that she was going to the funeral.

Realising that this was a battle she was not going to win Bridget took a different approach. She informed Mam that apart from her, no one attending Mollie's funeral knew that Mam was Mollie's daughter – none of her siblings, extended family, friends or members of the Mallow community were aware of her existence. Bridget was also quick to point out that Mollie had been married to a local councillor,

Mam, aged about twenty-five.

John O'Sullivan, who had gone to his grave without ever knowing, and that his family, many of whom were in attendance, could not find out either. She finished off by telling Mam that for the sake of everybody, in particular Mollie, she must pull herself together at once and stop making a show of herself.

Mam's mother, Mollie. When I found this picture years later I understood why Bridget did not want Mam at Mollie's funeral – the physical resemblance between them was unmistakable.

I think that all of us sitting around the kitchen table found it impossible to believe Bridget's claim that nobody, apart from her, knew that Mollie had secretly given birth. Mollie and Mam had by now had a relationship for nearly a decade so it seemed almost implausible that Mollie never confided some detail of this to anybody other than Bridget. But there was something far more sinister at play here. The reality was, whether anybody else knew or not, this brutal and heartless dictation that Mam was receiving on the day of her mother's funeral was part of a bigger picture. What was taking place here was a remorseless, preventative measure by Bridget to ensure that her younger sister Mollie went to her grave untarnished by the disgrace of having given birth to a baby out of wedlock fifty years beforehand. And the most effective way to take this situation in hand was to callously unseat Mam from any notion she had of being recognised as Mollie's daughter.

And so, while Mam went to her mother's funeral, she was heartlessly shamed once more into keeping silent about her very existence. She did not sit in her rightful place as the daughter of Mollie at the front of the church with the chief mourners. She was not welcome. She and Phyllis sat where Bridget instructed them to, down the back of the church where Mam, the shameful family secret, could remain unseen.

Before Mam left Mallow she somehow had the strength left to make a request of Bridget – a secret request, one she felt could be afforded without any public embarrassment. Could she possibly have her mother's wedding band and the fur coat that she always wore?

This request was met with unbridled disdain from Bridget – she was keeping the fur coat herself and the wedding band had been buried with Mollie – end of story. But that was not the end of the story. Mam had checked before the coffin was closed and the wedding ring was not on her mother's finger. Yet Bridget deprived Mam, even in private, of recognition. This was too much for Mam to bear. Without any argument, she left Mallow and came back home to Dublin. To my knowledge she never returned there.

In the week after the funeral Mam made a small but significant recovery and it appeared that things might well return to normal soon. But unknown to any of us, this recovery was being bolstered by new hope Mam had about her mother. She had somehow convinced herself that everything that happened at the funeral was Bridget's doing and that in death Mollie would finally recognise Mam in her will. But when the will arrived, the final crushing blow was dealt to Mam by her own mother. Mollie left Mam £500 and as far as I can remember her house went to a niece and everything else she possessed went elsewhere. While not a wealthy woman, Mollie could have left Mam far more than £500. But there were far greater ramifications at stake for Mam than the amount she had been left. She had no interest in the money. All she craved was recognition, even if it only arrived with her mother's death.

The token amount left to Mam was a calculated move. If Mam had been left everything it would have revealed her as a person of far greater importance in Mollie's life than an occasional visitor, leaving some very embarrassing questions for her family to answer. On the other hand, if Mam had been left nothing she, as Mollie's only child, could have successfully contested the will, leading to the unavoidable disclosure of exactly who she was. It would be comforting to think that Mollie had been forced into this move, and considering Bridget's treatment of Mam, it was easy to imagine that Mollie probably came under some serious family pressure to make this decision.

Mollie was very young when she had had my Mam and at that time, in 1930s Ireland, it would have caused a huge scandal if it had been found out she was pregnant and had not given her child up. I could even understand Mollie not telling her husband. It must have been a huge strain to have kept Mam secret from him through all their married life. But what I couldn't understand was why Mollie had come back into Mam's life if she couldn't put things right, even at the end of her own life. Her husband was already dead and she had no other children to continue hiding this secret from. She had nothing to lose but her reputation by recognising Mam as her daughter.

I think that this was the most difficult thing for Mam to accept, that even in death Mollie had refused to recognise Mam as her only child. Mam had been rejected at birth by her mother and now she was experiencing the same cycle of rejection and abandonment all over again. All Mam had wanted was to be able to call Mollie her mother. She could, of course, have gone back to Mallow and shouted from the rooftops that she was Mollie's illegitimate daughter – it wasn't like any of us were going to stop her (myself and Da both offered to bring her back). But the Church and state had dealt with this possible outcome many years beforehand by carefully moulding Mam into the fearful adult she was when it came to the matters of her childhood. Mam would not force a family to recognise her. She had been taught to remain silent.

After this, Mam's mental health went from bad to worse. She tried desperately hard to keep everything together but her efforts were in vain. Soon she was unable to cope with everything she had been previously dealing with before Mollie's death. She became completely overwhelmed. She stopped socialising and spent much of her time alone at home. She began obsessing relentlessly over Mollie's wedding band and fur coat. Her moods would swing from erratic and high to terrifying lows, where she couldn't function on a basic level. Her mind was a prison, and she would obsess over the past, constantly changing her mind about what she believed to be true. Why had Bridget lied to her when she had seen for herself there was no ring on Mollie's finger? Or maybe she hadn't looked properly. Maybe Mollie had been buried with her ring. She would then spend days wondering what she had done wrong. Had it been her fault that her mother had rejected her?

She would tell herself that if she had been different, the outcome would have been different. Mam regressed into the rejected child she had once been and none of us could do anything about it.

Mam began to talk not only about the past in relation to Mollie but also about the three miscarriages she had suffered after I was born. This was when we all really started to worry. Mam rarely spoke about the miscarriages and certainly not in the terms she was using now. Two of the pregnancies had been very late in their term, between six and seven months. Mam now worried where her babies were buried or whether they had even been given a proper grave. She had been sent home from the hospital without having been allowed to see them and without being told what sex they were and now she wanted to know why. I sometimes wondered if Mam's anxieties about these miscarriages was guilt arising from the fear that she had abandoned those babies, just as she had been. Mam's thoughts had become a weapon against her, slowly destroying her. This was agony for her, and it was painfully hard on Da. Having to watch the woman he loved and adored fall deeper and deeper into a seemingly inescapable state of depression must have been unbearable for him. He went to work each day never knowing what he would come home to, and must have worried endlessly about what Mam might do to herself while he was gone. I think each of us was suffering from the effects of Mam's total collapse. Mam was the linchpin of the family, the person who kept everything going, and now she had fallen apart. As the months slipped by with no improvement, our hopes that she would recover were dwindling.

The night I arrived home and found Da sitting alone on the couch weeping was when I realised that things had really hit rock bottom. I had never once in my life seen Da crying and for all the tears that Mam had wept in recent months it was the tears my father shed that night that I found hardest to bear. He was in a situation that had rendered him useless to his wife – no matter how hard he tried, he quite simply didn't know how to help Mam break free from this dark place she was lost in. They were both as lost as each other now. I think

Mam and Da at a party in 1975. Mam had always said that marrying Da saved her, but after Mollie died, no matter how hard he tried, not even Da could make things right for her.

we both knew in that moment something had to be done – and that we were not the people to do it.

The next day Mam was brought to the doctor, who diagnosed her with being in the midst of a nervous breakdown. She was put on a heavy dose of antidepressants and while they numbed the pain of her broken heart and brought to a halt the dark thoughts that had invaded her mind since Mollie's death, they also had other unwanted effects. Mam became vacant, almost expressionless, and constantly tired, which brought with it a whole new set of problems. The smell of burnt potatoes and the sight of Mam lying on the couch now greeted me on my arrival home from school. Mam had lost all fight; she had been suppressed into silence and it had broken her.

I sat on the grass in the grounds of Kilmainham Hospital, thinking about the unnecessary suffering that Mam had been forced to endure and subsequently the pain our family had had to live with. Generations of pain, needlessly suffered. I suddenly found myself shivering from the damp that had gathered beneath where I sat. I got up, wondering if my shivers had been the ghost of a dead soldier passing through me or perhaps it was Mollie, who in death was suffering an uneasy sleep.

Mollie may well have been effectively still a child when she gave birth to Mam and Mam may have been a grown woman by the time they finally met, but in those moments when they were together, Mam was the child who needed reassurance and Mollie was the parent who could provide it. In these moments, my heart broke for the little girl Mam once was. I thought of this small innocent being, rejected for circumstances beyond her control, deemed lesser from birth and then sent to live at the notoriously abusive industrial school in Goldenbridge, all the while promising herself that someday soon her mother would come to get her. Mam suffered her rejection and abandonment as a baby only to relive it decades later. Mollie's parting gift to Mam was the affirmation that she would never belong to someone.

Any anger that I had felt towards Mam back in the house had by now dispersed. As I walked back to our home my heart felt full of sorrow for her but my mind was swamped with frustration at the Establishment and the Irish structures that had moulded her and so many innocent other born in similar circumstances into the broken and fearful people they were now.

Mam and I might always clash, but I returned home with the resolve to be more patient with her.

11

Holes in his Boots

The media were a crucial lifeline in highlighting our strike and gaining public support, and one we utilised whenever possible. Within days of the Special Branch officer targeting Theresa Mooney at her home, we informed the press of the garda harassment towards us, both on and off the picket line. While we didn't achieve the big headlines we had hoped for, we did manage to get some press inches that were sympathetic in tone.

This media attention must have filtered back to Government Buildings because, soon after, we heard that more questions were being asked in the Dáil as to why no efforts to resolve our strike were being made. At that time, there was a Fine Gael/Labour coalition in power. Fine Gael were notoriously anti-strike but some of the more left-leaning progressive members of the Labour Party were becoming increasingly vocal, not only about our strike but also why we, as a country, were in effect funding the inhumane apartheid system by buying in the produce of their slave labour? People like Michael D. Higgins and Brendan Ryan were still pointing out that this was not an

A 1985 march in support of the Dunnes Stores strikers (© Derek Speirs).

industrial dispute but that it was, in fact, a political issue that could only be solved by the government.

The voices raising concerns within the Dáil were, however, still very much in the minority and we needed someone from the top table in our corner. But at this stage, despite the many letters asking for help and a growing concern both inside and outside of Government Buildings, Ruairi Quinn, the Minister for Labour, was sticking firmly to his position that his hands were tied: this was an industrial dispute and he could not intervene.

We debated disputing the findings of the garda investigation but if the Minister for Justice was saying there was no evidence of any wrongdoing, what was the point? In him, we had reached the pinnacle of power and there was nowhere further that we could go. We also knew that focusing our attention on a situation we were powerless to resolve was futile.

Dunnes Stores management had by now devised a completely new way of getting South African produce into the store. They were employing the services of Murray's Carriers – a rubbish disposal company – to sneak the South African goods into the Henry Street Store undetected inside their bin trucks. It was impossible for us to know how long this had been happening, but when we found out we were certain it was a story we could get onto the front pages. We informed the press and they, with due diligence, followed up the story. Nearly every newspaper ran the story and most publications ran pictures of Ben Dunne with some comical headlines. Within twenty-four hours the Health and Safety inspectors were called in. It would have been good to think that they could have brought an end to this clearly unhygienic way of transporting goods but it wasn't the case. For reasons we will never know, the investigation by the Health and Safety inspectors quietly and rather inexplicably went away, and for the rest of the strike Murray's bin trucks continued to be the main means of delivery of South African goods for Dunnes Stores.

In spite of this apparent victory on his part, you couldn't help but wonder how Ben Dunne was feeling privately about this unwanted media attention. A few days later, John Mitchell told us of a phone call he had just received from Dunne, informing him that as long as the law allowed South African goods in Ireland, the produce would remain on the shelves of every branch of Dunnes Stores and every shopworker would be expected to handle them. We should have known that this bull-headedness would be the response.

Winter closed in on us, and brought with it new problems we had not yet had to consider. It was a cruel winter, the worst in forty years, arriving with winds that whipped through your bones and never-ending sleets of freezing-cold snow. Physically and mentally, we were exhausted. We began to ask the question: how long could we carry on like this? But as the flus and colds reached epidemic levels on the picket line it was our supporters and our families who again stepped in with kindness and reinforcements when we needed them most. During the worst weeks they would bring endless changes of clothes and hot food, which stoked the fire in our hearts and kept us determined. Karen Gearon lived not far from the picket line and, during breaks, her mam, Joan, who was hugely supportive of the strike, welcomed us all into her home to get some much-needed warmth and replenishment for the next shift. At the end of our gruelling shifts, Theresa Mooney's husband, Brendan, would arrive in his van to collect the placards that hung from our weary shoulders. We would usually store the placards in Buckley's Butcher on Moore Street. The shopkeepers in Buckley's would always welcome us in with a fresh pot of tea. It was these moments of kindness and kinship that made the bitter days bearable.

We found other ways of beating the cold on the severest of days – snowball fights! I think the fun we were having outside must have got to our colleagues working away inside the shop because one day we heard a few of them calling down from the canteen window. They wanted to know what we thought they should spend their Christmas bonus on. We said nothing. We just waited patiently and when they were back at their tills we pushed open the front entrance began firing the pile of snowballs we had prepared for them through the front door. For the rest of that day a manager had to stand guard by the shop door and after that we never heard mention of their Christmas bonuses again.

These long, harsh days were, in some ways, the toughest we had faced so far but support was growing and sometimes on a Saturday there would be up 300 people standing with us on the picket line.

In spite of the weather Nimrod arrived still every single day without fail. His arrival each morning was a sight that never ceased to amaze me, particularly during the harsher weather. It was Tommy who first noticed that the soles of Nimrod's leather boots were holed – the same pair he had worn since the day he joined us on the picket line and they were now beyond repair. Once Tommy mentioned it, none of us could ignore it. Nimrod was out on this picket line completely of his own volition, and he was silently suffering because of it. We decided to club together and buy him a new pair of boots. I will never forget the day Tommy presented Nimrod with the brand-new pair of leather boots. It was hard to say if he was embarrassed or just overwhelmed but it was clear that this was a man not used to receiving anything. But I saw something in Nimrod's eyes. It was as though we had reminded him that, even though evil was prevailing while the apartheid government remained in charge, there was still kindness and caring in this world too. We never mentioned it again, and neither did he, but from that day on we never saw Nimrod's old boots again.

The inaction from everybody with the power to end our dispute was beginning to have an undermining effect, resulting in a stalemate on the picket. Ben Dunne was still insisting that all correspondence regarding the dispute be directed to his management at the Henry Street branch but in turn all of our requests to meet with them were being completely ignored. Ben Dunne remained firm in his stance that as long as it was legal to sell South African goods, he would stock them, going as far as to suggest that if he started banning goods based on countries that it could lead to demands to ban goods from Britain with whom Ireland had a fractious relationship with at the time due to the Troubles in the North.

The Irish government still maintained that they could not intervene. The view now being taken was that this was an issue of conscience and if a conscience law were to be passed, it could open up a conversation on abortion. It was becoming increasingly clear to us now that both the government and Dunnes Stores were willing to use any pretext, including very contentious issues of the time, in order excuse their inaction regarding our dispute. It was probably hoped that, if ignored long enough, this problematic issue would disappear off their agenda. We were six months into the strike and I think we all knew it was time to step up our campaign. We weren't going backwards but our moves forward were not bold enough to bring about any real change. We needed to shift up a gear and and broaden the scope of our strategies.

Since Nimrod arrived on the picket he had often spoken about a South African , an Anglican bishop by the name of Desmond Tutu, who had risen to prominence in recent years for his vigorous and unequivocal opposition to apartheid both in South Africa and abroad. Often comparing the regime to Nazism, Tutu had, in many ways, become the greatest thorn in the side of the apartheid government and, as a result, they had twice revoked his passport in efforts to prevent him from spreading his message to the outside world.

What really set Desmond Tutu apart from other political activists and opponents of the apartheid regime was that he renounced violence as a means to achieve political freedom – this and his growing international reputation is what protected him from any reprisal from the increasingly frustrated South African government. They had also learnt the hard way from their brutal dealings with Steven Biko and Nelson Mandela that a dead or imprisoned icon is far more dangerous than a live and free one.

Tutu vigorously opposed the policies of Western governments that continued to advocate 'friendly persuasion' as a method of dealing with the repugnant regime – and he made no effort to hide his dissatisfaction with foreign governments' handling of the matter. Without fear of retaliation, he continually highlighted the lack of outrage or even empathy from the West at the wanton destruction and demoralisation of human life in his homeland. Ultimately, his belief was that only a global economic boycott of his country could lead to the end of apartheid rule. But, as is often the case, the pillars of most evil – money and power – had the upper hand. While Western governments were trying to be seen to make efforts to distance themselves from the regime, which was becoming increasingly repellent to the wider world, they were unwilling to deny themselves the abundant supply of gold, diamonds, coal and food produce that South Africa continued to provide at a very cheap cost.

We had known of Tutu's name and his objectives for a while, but by the winter of 1984 he was drawn to our attention in a far bigger way. After being nominated in 1981, 1982 and 1983, he was finally announced in 1984 as the winner of the Nobel Peace Prize. Although our action was only a comparatively very small one, we were doing exactly what Desmond Tutu was looking for: boycotting the sale of South African goods. We now wondered if there was any way that we contact this man to see if he would make a public statement of support that might bring us one step closer to achieving our goal. We began asking around. There was an organisation called Afri, whose members were by now regulars on the picket line, and their goal was the promotion of global justice and peace, and high on their agenda was the South African situation. It was decided that any approach made by us would be more effective if made through them.

A letter was sent by Afri to Desmond Tutu on our behalf, explaining the background to our action, detailing the efforts we were making and the predicament we now found ourselves in with regards to our employer, the Irish government and the majority of the Irish Establishment. None of us really expected a reply, if he even received our letter at all. This was a man who had just won the Nobel Peace Prize and we felt he would be far too busy to have time for our little local action but we couldn't have been more wrong.

About a week later I was up in my bedroom dozing after another long day on the picket line when Da shouted up the stairs, 'Hey, Mary. Brendan Archbold is on the phone for you.'

We had no home phone in those days so any phone calls for us came to our neighbour's house two doors down. I clambered out of bed and walked up the road half asleep. It was hard to say how I felt when Brendan told me I should pack my bags, because Karen and I were going to London to meet Bishop Desmond Tutu. I just remember going back into my house and breaking the news to Mam and Da.

Da was delighted. He could immediately recognise the benefits of this for our strike action. But Mam was totally confused. She kept saying, 'You're going to meet a bishop? Why are you going to meet a bishop? He's the bishop of where?'

In spite of being deeply religious Mam had never heard of

Desmond Tutu, but she was highly impressed that I was off to meet a bishop and now wondered what I should wear. As Mam tortured herself over outfit choices for me I tried to get my head around the whole unfolding of events where a man with as international a reputation as Bishop Desmond Tutu wanted to meet us. The one thing that was obvious to me now was that his dedication to freeing his country from the shackles of the apartheid regime were so deep rooted that he was willing to take any support, no matter how small it was, from wherever it came.

That night I lay in bed, unable sleep a wink. I felt nervous about what lay ahead and my mind was swimming with notions about what to expect. However, I also felt a seed of hope within me. The resilience, perseverance and strength that I had developed over the first few months of the strike had been weathered and beaten down by these tough winter months and I would be lying if I said there weren't moments where I felt completely in despair. But hope can completely change a situation, especially when it arrives unexpectedly and from the unlikeliest of places. Maybe nothing would come of meeting Bishop Tutu but when I finally drifted off to sleep, it was with the comfort that this could well be a crucial moment for us and for our strike.

12

Meeting Tutu

On 8 December 1984, Karen Gearon, Brendan Archbold and I departed Dublin on the Sealink ferry and sailed across the Irish Sea to Holyhead. From there, Brendan drove us the 300 miles to London. Our destination was Heathrow Airport where Bishop Desmond Tutu was on a brief stopover while travelling from South Africa to Oslo, where he was to be presented with the Nobel Peace Prize. Although unintentional, the timing of our request for a statement of support from Desmond Tutu couldn't have been more fortunate. It had prompted the hastily arranged invitation to meet him in London.

We entered the airport and were shown into a small room where we were asked to wait. I had no idea what to expect. The fact that I was about to meet a Nobel Peace Prize winner was so far outside my wildest imaginings it was hard to believe it was really happening. Only the day beforehand we had been on the picket line receiving our daily dose of abuse. Karen was equally anxious. We kept shifting from very serious conversations about what would be most appropriate to say when Tutu entered the room to bursting into nervous fits of laughter. My apprehension realistically arose from all my previous interactions with any member of a religious order. Priests and nuns in Ireland had such an air of authority and grandeur that I found them intimidating. So it came as a complete shock when Tutu arrived through the door, an energetic man, arms open and smiling.

Bishop Desmond Tutu greeted us with a huge hug, full of warmth and kindness and without the slightest air of superiority. He thanked us profusely for our action, which he described as unprecedented, telling us that he knew of no other action in history where people had gone out on strike for an issue outside their own country and praised us for lifting the morale of millions of South African people. It is hard to describe exactly how I felt at that moment – on one hand Tutu was so welcoming and sincere that he put me at complete ease but on another hand the words he spoke were so humbling and emotive. Within two minutes of meeting, this hugely powerful and influential man had given us more validation than anybody in power in Ireland had since the beginning of our action.

Desmond Tutu then took the time to ask us in meticulous detail about our strike – how it had started and how it was going now. We were honest and admitted that it was difficult and often a struggle, to which he expressed no surprise. He explained, quite simply, that his own experience had shown him that when it came to pitting issues of conscience against economic gain this was normally the outcome. More often than not, money and power outweighed the value of human life, and his homeland was a stark and depressing example of this. After roughly twenty minutes of intense conversation, Tutu told us he would like to hear more but admitted that he had a prearranged press conference he must attend and asked if we would like to come and watch it.

At the press conference, I began to comprehend what this day was really about. There were hundreds of news and press reporters present, and when Tutu entered the room it became ablaze with flashbulbs. Karen and I stood to the side of the room (Brendan preferred to keep to the background) and watched as Bishop Desmond Tutu launched into a masterclass on how to stir the conscience and the heart. His message was clear – all global business dealings that aided and abetted the brutal South African regime had to cease. As I gazed around the room full of captivated men and women, journalists from all over the world, furiously jotting down in their notepads every word that Tutu spoke, it struck me that Tutu had made a clever move by having his press conference in London. He was ensuring that today was not about his Nobel Peace Prize win at all, but about shining a light firmly on South Africa.

In 1984 the enormously powerful and prominent relationship between US President Ronald Reagan and British Prime Minister Margaret Thatcher was at its height; economic sanctions, if they were ever to come, would most likely be a joint decision from both the US and British governments. This, in turn, would almost guarantee that the rest of the Western world, the main consumers of South African goods, would follow suit. Desmond Tutu knew that the only way to sway those in power was to pressure them through public opinion, and the best way to get public opinion on his side was through the media. The timing of his press conference was to guarantee that international headlines carried this message of shame and embarrassment to all those who chose to turn a blind eye, and thus receiving his award in Oslo would not overshadow the real issue at hand.

What happened next demonstrated to me the genius of this man, and allowed me to fully comprehend why he was such an imposing threat to his own government. Tutu called for me and Karen to join him. Suddenly we were standing in front of hundreds of cameras blinding us with their continuous flashing. Tutu explained our action to the room, commending it and then demanded that all Western governments should not only support our action, but do the same as us, because an economic embargo was the only way to bring the apartheid regime to its knees. Tutu then turned his tactics of shaming and embarrassing the beneficiaries of the apartheid regime on Ben Dunne, by stating that he, as an employer, should be proud to have people like us working for him. I smiled to myself, imagining Ben Dunne's face as he read this in the newspaper the next morning.

The atmosphere in the room was electric and the moment was surreal for us: here we were, two striking shopworkers, being publicly congratulated by one of the most influential people on the planet. And despite the incredulity that gripped me, in that moment it was clear what Tutu was doing with Karen and me – it was profoundly clever, yet simple. By highlighting to the international press an action that had been taken by an ordinary group of working-class people for the ordinary but beleaguered black South Africans, he was bypassing the governments and the decision makers, and using his influence to connect our story to ordinary people all around the world. In one masterstroke, he used this moment to try to sway the public, to bring them together as one voice, opposing a situation they would all view as wrong. They could inevitably become a policy-changing force. The aim was ambitious and came from a very small place but it held both possibility and hope. Two words that terrified those in power.

Once my disbelief and astonishment settled, I stood at the top of that room and wished more than anything that all those back in Ireland who had opposed our action from the very start were here today, with Karen and myself. I would defy every one of them not to be moved by what Bishop Desmond Tutu was saying. I could feel a surge of anger building as I thought about how they were misusing their power: Ben Dunne, his management, the Irish government, the Garda Síochána, Bishop Eamonn Casey, the Catholic Church, Kader Asmal, our own union

Bishop Desmond Tutu, winner of this year's Nobel Peace Prize with Ms Mary Manning, a striking worker from Dunne's store in London yesterday.—(UPI wirepicture; report: page 5)

A newspaper photo of my meeting with Desmond Tutu in 1984.

129

executive – all those on the ever-expanding list were so preoccupied with keeping the status quo, they didn't stop to consider the ramifications this could have on millions of lives. If they had witnessed what we just had – a compelling, passionate and highly articulate argument from a deeply religious man opposed to any form of violence and terrorism – how could any one of them, in good conscience, justify their continued stance against us and our action? Perhaps if they had been present, maybe even just one of them would have had the courage to stand up and say, yes, there was something fundamentally wrong here, and if we joined forces we could rectify this appalling situation. A law could be pushed through at once that banned the sale of South African goods in Ireland, one that would allow us to go back to work and let Ireland be seen as a progressive country that had the nerve to stand up and say no to what was so clearly wrong, a ruthless regime that enslaved over 20 million impoverished black South Africans.

That one meeting in London changed everything. Bishop Desmond Tutu had given us an international focus and we arrived back to the picket line knowing that we were no longer a brave little protest on one shopping street in Dublin. This may have started with a shop cashier asking a shopper to set two South African Outspan grapefruits aside but it was about to have far-reaching effects, much farther than Henry Street.

That first Saturday after our meeting with Tutu, people began showing up at the picket line and they kept coming. By late afternoon it was impossible to tell how many were there because the crowds stretched far beyond where the eye could see. We were no longer counting hundreds of supporters – it was now thousands. The public's perception of what we were doing had changed overnight because a Nobel Peace Prize winner had articulated the importance of what we were doing and suddenly people were focusing on why we were actually out there on the street picketing.

We now had more public support than we could have imagined and soon well-known faces began to appear. John Hume travelled from Derry, and Tony Benn and striking coal miners flew in from the

Support was building, particularly on Saturdays, when people were off work. Even if shoppers wanted to go into Dunnes Stores on Henry Street they could never get past the crowds protesting outside it (Rose Comisky).

UK to rally support for us. Christy Moore came to sing songs while Seamus Heaney turned up to read poetry for the gathered crowds. We started to receive messages of support internationally from the likes of Edward Kennedy and Jesse Jackson. Meanwhile, all was silence from Dunnes Stores management and the Irish government. While this frustrated us, we decided not to let it weigh on our minds too much. While Dunnes Stores could continue to dig their heels in, we knew at some point the government, which relied on public support to keep it in power, would have to break – remaining silent throughout such a public outcry would eventually work against it.

Christmas came and went and public support remained firm. By January 1985, this and the increasing complaints from minority voices

Poets Seamus Heaney *(right)* and Hugh Maxton on the Dunnes Stores picket line in protest against the hanging of the South African poet Benjamin Moloise (© Derek Speirs).

in government could no longer be ignored by those at the top table. Ruairi Quinn made a public demand that Dunnes Stores engage in immediate talks with our union in the Labour Court to resolve the dispute. At once our union moved to set up a meeting.

On the other hand, we on the picket line made a decision that no matter what promises were being made, it was essential that we keep up the momentum on the picket. Previous experience had shown us from day one that actions spoke far louder than words, so rather than rely on this one meeting, which could take weeks to arrange, we decided that keeping the pressure up would be far more advantageous in moving towards our goal.

While our anti-apartheid strike was making advances in Ireland, the miners' strike in the UK was suffering significantly at the hands of Margaret Thatcher and her ruthless determination to break the trade unions at any cost. In an effort to rally support for their predicament and also highlight our action, an invitation came in for two of us to make a speaking tour around the UK at trade union meetings, universities, schools and anti-apartheid rallies. I think we all realised the importance of an invitation like this because it was no longer just about us as shopworkers being granted the right not to handle South African goods, it was about trying to get a much wider message across about the necessity of a global ban on South African produce, and reinforcing to as many people as possible that this was what black South Africans wanted. If this invitation had arrived earlier in our strike we could not have taken it up as it took all ten of us to man the three entrances of the Dunnes Stores Henry Street branch but, with the increased public support on a daily basis, we were now being afforded time away from the picket line.

The tour was to take nearly a month. It was decided that Cathryn O'Reilly and I would go on what would prove to be an eye-opening and sometimes difficult journey. In particular, the places we visited in northern England and Scotland where whole communities, whose very survival was dependent on the coal-mining industry, suffered from extreme hardship, hunger, lack of fuel and levels of police violence we had never endured on our picket line. By January 1985, Margaret Thatcher's efforts to brand hard-working miners as the 'enemies of democracy' had made huge grounds during the tough winter months so even at that stage, well before they and their union were finally bulldozed into submission, the toll on these communities was both horrifying and heartbreaking to see.

At the other end of the spectrum, the talks at the universities and anti-apartheid rallies that we attended were completely inspirational and hugely motivating. It was about three weeks into our UK tour when something happened that escalated support for the anti-apartheid movement worldwide. The South African government had been coming under mounting international pressure since Tutu's Nobel Peace Prize win to take some definitive action to appease the growing opposition to their political system. On 31 January 1985, in an effort to quell their critics, South African Prime Minister P. W. Botha offered Nelson Mandela conditional release. The condition was that he and the ANC renounce violence and violent protest as a means to bring about change in South Africa. Mandela immediately spurned the offer, and communicated his refusal through a poignant and provoking statement read out by his daughter Zindzi at a rally in Soweto the following week. In it, Mandela described violence as the responsibility of the apartheid regime; with democracy there would be no need for it. He also questioned the type of freedom he was being offered when the very organisation he and his people were part of, the ANC, remained banned. For the first time in twenty-one years the world heard the words of an imprisoned icon who, despite years of incarceration, still refused to compromise his political goals in order obtain his freedom. The apartheid government had done nothing but stoke the fire and during our final days in the UK, every rally we attended started and ended to the crowds chanting 'Free Nelson Mandela'.

Back on the picket line, Nelson Mandela's potent words of warning to his oppressors, that there was no freedom for one man without freedom for all, was having the same profound effect in Ireland as Cathyrn and I had witnessed in the UK. The South African government, as it had done with Bishop Desmond Tutu, had yet again completely underestimated the power of the spoken word against their regime. Nelson Mandela and Desmond Tutu were two men with the same vision of freedom for their country with entirely opposing views on how to achieve it but both making huge gains against the regime they detested.

The pavement outside Dunnes Stores on Henry Street was now the place where anybody in Ireland opposed to apartheid came to let their feelings be known. The tide of public opinion was turning at such speed none of us on the picket line could have anticipated it. Only months beforehand we were lucky to get through a day without at least one of us being referred to as a 'nigger lover'. Now people young and old were arriving daily, some holding photos of a youthful and charismatic Nelson Mandela, and others held pictures of the brutally slain activist Steve Biko.

Now, more than ever, it felt that anything was possible. Very soon after this we were approached by a man on the picket line who said that Bono would like to meet us and talk about our action. As this invitation was to go to Windmill Lane Studios, only a stone's throw from our picket line, there was no discussion as to who should go: we all piled into three taxis he ordered for us and off we went.

Bono arrived late and spent the first ten minutes apologising profusely to us for his tardiness, explaining that his car had broken down on the way. We discussed with him in detail what we were trying to achieve and he promised us that he would do all he could to highlight our action. Before we left he also offered us some advice as to how we should deal with times of adversity. Brushing his hand through his fringe, he said to us, in a way that only Bono could: 'Be angry. Don't be bitter, be angry.' There was no way that he could have known this, but for months afterwards we impersonated this moment on and off the picket line. If something happened we didn't like or we were just a bit bored of the never-ending circling of the Dunnes Stores entrance, one of us would inevitably run their fingers through their fringe and say to the rest of us, 'Be angry. Don't be bitter, be angry.'

The Catholic Church had yet to voice any support, which in many ways surprised me, particularly after our meeting in London with Bishop Desmond Tutu, which had garnered headlines all over the world. This must have put them into an awkward position, particularly Bishop Eamonn Casey and the private but very damning stance he had taken against us. At this stage I could only imagine that he, never having envisaged that our action would gain so much public support, must have regretted putting his feelings down on paper. But the day that nuns started arriving on the picket line we knew that somebody somewhere must have been feeling the heat. These nuns, who only months beforehand had passed our picket in a flurry of heinous accusations that our action was starving impoverished black South Africans, now joined us on the picket line, declaring to anybody who would listen that what we were doing should be commended. We wouldn't deny their support. At this stage we would take help from wherever it came. At the time, we all believed their arrival must have been motivated by the men at the top of their organisation. We had been so stung by their original reaction that it was hard for us to step back and see the bigger picture, which was that we, in educating ourselves about the issue and shining the media spotlight on it, had in turn educated and influenced the Irish public in a positive way. We now felt sure it was only a matter of time before the stance of the Church would have to sway in our favour.

As the winter chill gave way to spring there was a new air of positivity on the picket line. It seemed to us that there was nothing anybody could do, no matter how powerful they were, to stop this already moving train from ploughing full steam out of the station.

13

The Wedding Band and
the Match Box

On 7 March 1985, during the launch of Trócaire's Lenten campaign, Bishop Eamonn Casey made a public U-turn on his position regarding our action. During a televised speech, he commended us and stated that the Dunnes Stores strike deserved the respect and solidarity of all Irish people. This was the most public statement of support we could receive. While it was met with a good deal of cynicism by us on the picket line, we kept this to ourselves. Bishop Eamonn Casey was a powerful and influential man so accepting his support was not optional – even if it had been coerced through the awkward situation Bishop Desmond Tutu had placed him in.

As good as his word, Bono had also made a statement of support for our action within days of us meeting him. A few weeks later he took his backing of the strike even further. Three taxis arrived on the picket line and we were asked if we would go back to Windmill Lane Studios where Bono was recording his contribution to the album *Artists Against Apartheid* with the song 'Sun City'. Less than an hour later we, the strikers, were all in the recording studio with headphones on, recording as the backing singers for Bono. Speaking for myself, I would say that singing was not one of my finer talents and I would imagine it took a good deal of retuning to fix the track after we left. There were many difficult days on the picket line but it was days like this that broke the monotony and lifted our spirits, particularly as the weeks drifted by and we found ourselves in April without much having changed.

There had been a vocal outpouring of support after we had met Tutu in London, including from the Irish government, which had made statements about how appalling and unacceptable apartheid was. While it was clear to see on a daily basis that the public were with us, there had, for some time, been a disconcerting silence from the Irish government and the Labour Court in regard to getting Dunnes Stores to negotiate. So the fact remained that the only people who could end the dispute were still not willing to put their words into action.

In another worrying turn of events, word came back from Brendan Archbold that support within our union was wavering further. They were completely unsympathetic towards our situation and there was now a growing desire to bring an end to the matter, regardless of how it was achieved. Apparently, the very conservative hierarchy within the union were unimpressed by the 'goings-on' at the picket line and now wondered how much longer they could take our action seriously when we were clearly having so much 'craic'. While there were moments that great things were happening for us, these were outweighed by the personal difficulties we were all experiencing. As more weeks slipped by without a sign of a meeting that could even begin negotiations, the financial implications on all of us were a huge strain, one that was being transferred to our families.

There was also another issue that had knocked the confidence of all of us on the picket line. In early March, the National Union of Miners, the most powerful union in the UK, had succumbed to the onslaught from Thatcher's Conservative government and called off

At a photocall in March 1984 (l–r): Tommy Davis, Cathryn O'Reilly, Sandra Griffin, me, Alma Russell, Theresa Mooney, Vonnie Monroe with her daughter Leah and Karen Gearon (© Derek Speirs).

their strike. While our strike was very different in nature, their outcome was having an unavoidable undermining effect on ours, leaving us with the concern that if the huge public support and the bright light that Tutu had shone on our action couldn't help bring about change, what possibly could? While on the surface it had appeared to us that the end was in sight, this was not the case. In fact, another letter from Minister for Labour Ruairi Quinn to John Mitchell proved this beyond doubt. While we had made huge steps in advancing our campaign, no such efforts were being made inside Government Buildings. Having discussed it at cabinet, the Government agreed it was still not in a position to intervene in an industrial dispute. This news really brought it home to us that we were nowhere near the end, and now, more than ever, it seemed that the gap between the strikers and the Establishment was widening.

I tried to remain positive, but as the momentum gained by Tutu began to wane, and our own situation became more precarious, it

(L–r): Liz Deasy and me leaving a meeting in late March 1985. At this stage we had the support of the public and many well-known figures but without any action from the Irish government, it was hard not to worry where it all might end (© Derek Speirs).

was becoming impossible to envision how this this David-and-Goliath tale could have a happy ending. But then, as had happened so often during our strike, something completely unpredicted occurred and changed the course of our action. In the form of a telegram, a new situation arose, swinging the ball firmly back into our court, and from the very man who only a few months beforehand had supplied us with a surge of support: Bishop Tutu. The telegram, from Bishop Desmond Tutu and the South African Congress of Churches, was addressed to Mr Ben Dunne and the Dunnes Stores Strikers. It was an invitation for all of us to travel to South Africa,

A newspaper report on Bishop Tutu's invitation.

Tutu invites Ben Dunne to S.A.

By CHRISTINE NEWMAN

IN a surprise development in the eight-month-old Dunnes Stores anti-apartheid dispute, both the strikers and the owner of the stores chain, Mr. Ben Dunne, have been invited to South Africa by Nobel Peace Prize winner, Bishop Desmond Tutu.

The invitation was also extended by the general secretary of the South African Council of Churches, Dr. Beyers Naude, and was sent via the Action from Ireland group in Dublin.

The Bishop and Dr. Naude said in a telegram sent to the group that all concerned in the

where Desmond Tutu would personally bring us to the townships where we could witness at first hand the atrocities of the apartheid regime. After nine months on the picket line we were all overwhelmed at the thought that we might actually get to meet the people we were striking for.

Throughout the Dunnes Stores Strike Brendan Archbold fastidiously made copies of all important correspondence that came in and passed them round to each of the strikers on the picket line for the duration of the strike. Of all the copies of correspondence he gave me – and by the time the strike finished it had run into hundreds – it was the copy of Tutu's telegram that I remember most clearly, and not just because of its contents, but because of how my Mam reacted when I showed it to her.

That evening while we ate dinner, the telegram was passed around kitchen table. I felt some pride as each family member read it with excitement, but my stomach dropped when the telegram finally came to Mam. When she took it in her hand she became quite emotional. I even noticed a small tremor to the side of her mouth and a pained expression took hold of her features.

At once, I was reminded of the day when me and my Mam sat at our kitchen table, nine months after Mollie had died, both equally overwhelmed by what had arrived in the post that morning. It was a moment that had changed the course of Mam's life, the one that probably saved her.

In the first few months after Mam had been medicated she

never made mention of Mollie, the wedding band, the fur coat, her lost babies or anything at all for that matter. Mam was a silent spectre, drifting through the house like the ghost of the woman she had been. The constant smell of burnt food from the kitchen and the piles of unwashed clothes on our upstairs landing were small but constant reminders that Mam was out of it most of the time. I noticed that, after a while, she began to even out somewhat. She was still nowhere near her old self but she began to talk about Mollie and the ring again, the only difference being that now she would forget what she was saying and drift off to another subject before getting to the point. So while they may have lowered her medication or her body was just now used to it, I knew by her subdued and often weary demeanour she was still on something and it was doing the job it was meant to do: to block out her pain. I guess the greatest difficulty for us as a family was that it blocked out every other aspect of Mam's personality too, the parts we loved so much. There was no laughter in our house any more and I longed for the sounds of 'the women' cackling in our sitting room. Mam was only a shell of the woman she had once been. She had lost her will to carry on.

Nowadays, I hope, more could have been done to help Mam, but Ireland was still locked in the vice-like grip of total denial about its treatment of unmarried mothers and their unwanted babies. So to even suggest that Mam needed help to cope with what had happened to her as a child, added to the subsequent trauma she was forced to go through as an adult, was futile – it was never going to be recognised by any professional in that era. It was one of those times when you're expected to suffer in silence, and that's what we all did in the Manning household until that morning I found myself sitting at our kitchen table opposite my Mam.

Between us was a small package, addressed to her and it had arrived wrapped in brown paper. She opened it and within the brown paper was a matchbox. When Mam pushed the matchbox open she pulled out a piece of old newspaper, frayed at the edges, and from that Mollie's gold band fell out. That was the day we as a family began to see Mam walk the road to recovery back towards being the person we all knew and loved. I'd be lying if I said it was like a light bulb switched on and she was miraculously cured. Like all ailments of the mind, heart and soul, it was a slow process and it wasn't a linear progression of healing. She had good days and bad days. But when that band of gold fell out on our kitchen table, I saw something spark within her. I believe it was hope. A simple band of gold was all it was, meaningless to anyone else, but it gave Mam the validation she had so long yearned for. In my Mam's mind now this ring had been bestowed to her by her mother, Mollie, although all evidence pointed to the contrary. I never cared or judged Mam for her blind belief. If this was what she needed to cope then I was just happy she had anything at all to cling to. She had been through enough.

I found out later that it was Da who got the ring for Mam. He had written several letters to Bridget in Mallow, none of which he had received a reply to. Then, as the months went by and knowing that Mam needed help before it became too late, Da got a number for Bridget and phoned her. I have no idea what he said to her but whatever he threatened, it was enough to make Bridget realise that not heeding Mam's request for her mother's wedding band would lead to an unwanted outcome – perhaps the very one that she had gone to all these lengths to avoid.

Mam never got Mollie's fur coat, and never mentioned it again. She didn't need to: Mollie's ring on her finger was enough. But when she recovered she soon reverted back to her old ways of telling me how Mollie had named her Josephine and how Mollie had never put her up for adoption. Mam had created her own narrative to protect her from the harsh realities that would have disabled her, once again, from living a normal happy life. Even back then I could recognise that there were many holes in Mam's story, but I also acutely aware that much of this came from Mam not knowing a good deal about it herself.

But, in many ways, Mam did get her happy ending. Within weeks of this matchbox being pushed through our front door Mam went to a jeweller's where she had Mollie's gold wedding ring melted into her own engagement ring. In that moment she bonded herself to her mother forever.

As I sat across the kitchen table, watching Mam anxiously thumb the invitation from Tutu, I could understand where her concern was coming from. I was going to embark on a journey that would take me to a country half a world away. A country where people were murdered each day, and words like justice, democracy and equal rights were merely a foreign concept. Mam had a right to be nervous. As did I. But I knew, sitting there, staring at Mam's concerned face, that I had inherited her bravery and her ability to never give up on even the faintest glimmer of hope. These were the traits that had got me through the strike so far and would get me through my journey to South Africa.

14

The Ordinary People of Ireland

Unsurprisingly, Ben Dunne never personally acknowledged the very public invitation from Bishop Desmond Tutu and the South African Congress of Churches, as undoubtedly he had no desire to travel to South Africa and take a guided tour of the horrors that were funding his expanding empire. 'No comment' was always the Dunnes Stores stance and it didn't waver in this situation.

We, of course, accepted the invitation immediately and decided to take the trip in July 1985 so that it would coincide with the first anniversary of our strike on 19 July. The first logistical problem to figure out was who would go. Up until this, invitations for us to travel generally come in for just one or two of us but this one was specifically for all of us. Because of this we decided that as many us as possible should go. We still had constant support on the picket line so it made it easier for the majority of us to go. Alma and Vonnie, for their own personal reasons, decided to stay at home and manage the picket while the rest of us wanted to travel to South Africa. The next challenge was the cost of the journey. We knew a trip of this scale would be expensive, but when we found out it the cost would be in or around £15,000 for the group, we knew the task ahead of us was much larger than any of us had anticipated.

In spite of John Mitchell and Brendan Archbold's best efforts, our union refused to contribute anything substantial towards the trip, which they described as a 'holiday to the sun'. A cheque for £500 was delivered to the picket line, which we believed was meant as a snub, but we were fiercely determined to make this journey and began to spend our time on the picket line trying to figure out how we could find the money. Our strike fund had nowhere near what we needed. The fund-raising events were helpful towards everyday bills, but only ever raised a nominal amount per event, so while a fund-raising event specially for the trip could contribute something, it would not be remotely enough. Something miraculous would need to happen in order for us to raise the funds needed. We knew this trip to South Africa was desperately needed for any future success the strike could achieve. Our last public meeting with Tutu had brought with it a wave of support, and this was only in London. A meeting with Bishop Desmond Tutu in the townships of Johannesburg where apartheid was dealing its worst blows would surely serve as the tipping point for the Irish government to take some proper action. We had been thrown a lifeline and needed to utilise it to best advantage. As we came up with various methods to raise funds, an unexpected obstacle emerged, blocking our way: Kader Asmal.

While the majority of the ordinary members of the Irish Anti-Apartheid Movement were still regulars on our picket line we had seen very little of Kader since he had asked us to end our strike six months beforehand. Then a letter arrived, proving that Kader Asmal was still not on board with our action. In the letter our visit to South Africa was described as 'a breach in the cultural embargo' and for this reason the IAAM could not be seen to support or finance the trip in any way. A cultural boycott on South Africa had been set up some years beforehand to deter or indeed embarrass music artists and sports people from taking up the lucrative deals that were on offer from South Africa during the apartheid regime. Most did not take advantage of this shameful way to make money but there were some who found it possible to turn a blind eye in order to a make a quick buck. It appeared to us that Kader was comparing us to those people. None of us could understand what this request for us not to travel to South Africa was motivated by.

About a week after the letter arrived, Brendan Archbold, along with a representative of Afri, the organisation that had made our initial introduction to Tutu, went to meet Kader Asmal at his house in Foxrock. It proved to be a very difficult meeting. On one side Kader maintained his argument that our trip was clearly a breach of the cultural embargo, while on the other, Brendan argued that the Dunnes Stores Strikers were hardly tourists invited to enjoy the finest South Africa had to offer, but clearly we were opponents of apartheid invited by one of the greatest and most respected opponents of apartheid. The aim of this invitation from Desmond Tutu was to embarrass the South African government, nothing else. Brendan also made the point that Senator Edward Kennedy had taken the exact same tour of the townships in South Africa only two months beforehand and nobody, including the United Nation, had accused him of breaking any embargo. In spite of all the argument, Kader was vehemently opposed to the trip, although to this day none of us knows why he objected so strongly. His argument made no sense to any of us. The meeting ended badly, with Brendan making it clear the only way the Dunnes Stores Strikers would be not travelling to South Africa was if Desmond Tutu cancelled the invitation. But before they left, it was mutually agreed that Kader's objections would be kept private so as to present a united front to the outside world.

As far as we strikers were concerned, this need to keep a 'united front' between ourselves and Kader Asmal was verging on the ridiculous. Pulling his support six months beforehand when we had little support had been a huge blow and if Kader had made his feelings public at that stage it could have had some serious fallout for us. But in those six months our strike had progressed hugely and any media exposure highlighting what Kader Asmal really thought of our action would, we felt, only result in bad press for everyone. Utimately, this would distract from the bigger issue so we agreed between us to simply dismiss his complaints and move forward.

With so much of the Establishment still unsupportive of our action there were very few places from where we could seek help. There was a contribution of £5,000 from an American supporter – this came through Afri and we were hugely grateful but we still needed £10,000. Small and much appreciated contributions came in from our supporters and charitable organisations, but by the end of May with our departure date looming closer, we were still nowhere near reaching our financial goal. One afternoon someone had the bright idea to buy a load of buckets and do a collection around Dublin. We applied for a permit to embark on a fund-raising mission and, surprisingly, we were granted it. The following Friday evening, all of us and a big number of our supporters descended on the Dublin pubs with our buckets in hand. We couldn't believe the reception we received. This was a country suffering a recession, where jobs were being lost and services slashed. We hadn't known what to expect, or how people would react to our request for help getting to South Africa, but the generosity of the Irish public that night was extraordinary. By the end of the night we had collected £7,500 and it was the ordinary people of Ireland who funded our trip to South Africa. The final money was then raised through fund-raising events helped by all sorts of Irish artists including Niall Toibin, Moving Hearts and Christy Moore.

It was a hugely inspirational and motivating period in our strike action to receive such goodwill from people who really didn't have much to give – and it proved to us how important the issue of apartheid had become to the ordinary Irish people. In the greater scheme of things the general public was not in a position to do much about this pitiless regime but it was these small actions from individuals that kept the home fires burning for us on Henry Street. While we delighted in what had happened, like most good things that

After a benefit concert in September 1985 for the Dunnes Stores Strikers (l–r): Davy Spillane, Keith Donald and Donal Lunny, who were all regulars on the picket line, me and Cathryn O'Reilly (© Derek Speirs).

happened on the picket line it was met with criticism from certain quarters, namely the executive of our union. At the next union meeting they questioned whether we really needed our £21 a week strike pay, if in one evening we had managed to raise enough funds to pay ourselves for nearly eight months. These condemnations of us were always made behind closed doors but they were the ones that hurt the most, particularly as they could not have been further from the truth. Each one of us was beyond broke at this stage – Vonnie, a single mother and the only homeowner among us, was on the verge of losing her home and there were many nights when I would stay with Karen, who lived nearby, because I quite simply didn't have the bus fare to get to and from the picket line. It was becoming increasingly difficult for us not to resent our union – these highly paid individuals who had issued the instruction that had put us into this situation in the first place. I wondered if any of them ever tried to imagine what we were going through on a daily basis. Did it never occur to any of them how easy it would be for us to swallow our pride, return to work and forget all about the apartheid regime and the millions of South Africans suffering under it? As far as I was concerned our union had taken advantage of an extraordinary act of generosity towards our action to take yet another cheap shot.

During this period of very positive publicity for the strike action Ben Dunne and his management remained ominously quiet. Then on 13 June 1985 a photograph of Ben Dunne attending the Bruce Springsteen concert in Slane Castle appeared in the Wigmore column of current affairs magazine *Magill*, which gave him exactly the type of publicity he went to great lengths to avoid.

It had all started two weeks beforehand when Theresa Mooney and I had gone to Slane Castle to collect free tickets that had kindly been offered to the strikers by the concert organiser, Lord Henry Mountcharles. But we had another reason for going there – we were both huge fans of Bruce Springsteen and we hoped to persuade Lord Mountcharles to let us meet him. He told us this would be impossible and, while we were a little disappointed, we were still delighted that we could even go. The concert was on 1 June, nearly a year into the strike, so it was heaven to escape the stresses of the picket line for one day. Theresa's husband, Brendan, borrowed a minibus and we sang Bruce's songs all the way there. I had never been to Slane before so to get inside, among the crowd of 80,000 people, was amazing. Once Bruce Springsteen came on, the place went wild and for the full three hours that he played, we danced and sang with everyone else.

We knew that Ben Dunne had been in the VIP section but what we didn't know was that our regular supporter and photographer on the picket line, Derek Speirs, had also been in this section and that he photographed him. The picture of the notoriously publicity shy Ben

Ben Dunne inside the VIP section at the Bruce Springsteen concert at Slane Castle, 1985 (© Derek Speirs).

Dunne enjoying a pint behind the high fencing of the VIP section appeared in the next issue of *Magill* accompanied by a short piece, which had been written by another supporter of our action, journalist Eamonn McCann. There were many down days on the picket line but that day in June 1985, when we read the article, we all fell around the place laughing.

> The corpulent man in the picture is Ben Dunne. He is the boss of Dunnes Stores. He is standing inside the white people's compound at the Springsteen concert in Slane. He had been

invited by Lord Henry Mountcharles. Also invited by Lord Mountcharles were the Dunnes Stores Strikers. But the strikers were not invited into the white people's compound. They were outside with the native masses.

From Magill, *13 June 1985*

15

South Africa

On the morning of 8 July Da and I left our house in Kilmainham for Dublin Airport. It was my twenty-second birthday and, as Mam waved me off, I wished more than anything that we had travelled on another date. Seeing me off on a trip she didn't want me to take, added to the occasion of my birthday, seemed to raise Mam's anxiety greatly.

It was a short drive to the airport and as the large, grey terminal building came into view, I couldn't help but think back to my twenty-first birthday. Little had I known then, as I sipped pints with my friends in my local pub, just how much my life would change in just one year – it was overwhelming. We arrived at the airport early and after I checked my suitcase I spotted Nimrod, standing quietly to the side. I went over and gave him a hug goodbye, but it was what he said next that made me realise Nimrod hadn't just come to see us off: he was concerned for us too. He said, 'If anything happens, Mary, remember not to make eye contact with anybody in authority.'

As always, Nimrod was to the point but I knew deep down that he was not saying this for dramatic effect. That was not his way. He was saying it because he knew better than any of us that authority in South Africa had a very different meaning than what we experienced in our everyday lives. Having witnessed us stand up and often rebel against authority in Ireland, I think Nimrod worried that this might have left us naïve to the reaction this kind of behaviour would receive from the South African police force. He was warning me that if there was any sign of trouble to keep my head down.

I went through the departure gates and waved back to Da. Standing just behind him was Nimrod, still smiling his reassuring, caring smile. It was in that moment I could not help but feel the cruel irony of this situation: Nimrod, born and raised in country he could not return to, and here we were, eight white Irish people about to embark on a journey to his homeland – a place where he would face certain death if he returned. His everyday existence was burdened with the knowledge that he might never set foot on South African soil again. He might never breathe in his native air or see his wife and four children again.

As I walked to our departure gate, my hatred of the apartheid regime burned in my core. The cruelty of denying someone the right to live a normal life because of the colour of their skin. I now recognised more deeply than ever what the Dunnes Stores strike actually meant to Nimrod. It was his lifeline, his connection to the hope that he might one day return to South Africa. The picket line was a place that afforded him some reprieve from a type of isolation that was inconceivable to us. In that moment I understood for the first time that Nimrod needed us just as much as we needed him, if not more.

Once the wheels hit the runway of Jan Smuts Airport and the plane came to a halt, I knew that there was no turning back. I was excited: this is what we had been planning for months and it was finally happening. Our trip to South Africa had so far been anything but smooth. We had landed London Heathrow from Dublin four hours before our connecting flight to Johannesburg was due to take off. Only moments after we checked in and our bags had gone through airport security, British Airways staff and a South African embassy representative descended on us, saying that we could not board the flight to South Africa. The embassy representative, Leo Evans, tried to insist that we needed a visa to go to South Africa, but this was untrue. Brendan Archbold, who was travelling with us, argued that Irish citizens did not need a visa to enter South Africa and legally we were within our rights to go. Although we had our tickets and our boarding passes, the British Airways staff asked us to come out to the tarmac and identify our bags. Again, we refused, delaying them even more, but soon it became obvious that no matter what delaying tactics we employed they were not going to let us board to the flight to South Africa under any circumstances. I tearfully rang Da from a payphone in the airport and told him that while our bags and all the journalists who had accompanied us were going to South Africa, we weren't. We would all be on the next flight back to Dublin. Da sounded disappointed for me and I know that he was being genuine, but I have to admit there was an undertone of relief in his voice.

But within minutes of my putting the phone down to Da, without any explanation whatsoever, suddenly everything changed. We were now all being hurriedly ushered towards the flight, which had already been delayed by three hours. When we boarded the flight all our seats had been reassigned so we could not seat with each other. I also noticed that we had entered a pretty hostile environment. When I took my seat beside a journalist from the UK, who was travelling over to cover our trip, he told me that the pilot had announced that the delay was due to a group of people who were refusing to board the flight – no wonder we were getting filthy looks from everyone.

I regret that I do not remember this journalist's name but he was very friendly and also was very curious to know what really had happened at the boarding gate. I explained it as best I could, for at this stage I myself had no idea what had brought on the sudden turnaround regarding our entry into South Africa. This journalist was a really lovely man and assured me that, as a regular traveller to and from South Africa, he knew that what had happened was not such an unusual occurrence at all. The apartheid government had become so paranoid about the increasing bad publicity that visitors were constantly being stopped or refused entry. Upon hearing that, I realised that we were very lucky to have got on the flight.

We exited the plane, exhausted but delighted by the welcome of the blaring sun. Nimrod had regaled us with vivid descriptions of the South African sky, but even his poetic storytelling paled in comparison to the real thing. It was a stunning, expansive sight and, as he had described, like no other. My eyes were diverted away from its beauty due to the commotion on the runway. I looked down towards the tarmac and saw there were maybe eighteen or twenty soldiers lined up on either side of the plane's stairs. I recognised them as South African Defence Forces (we had seen enough photos of South African soldiers in their camouflage uniform to know exactly who they were!). We guessed that there must have been someone pretty important on our flight to get a reception like this on arrival. I craned my neck as we descended, attempting to get a glimpse of who they were waiting for but when I reached the bottom step one of them directly demanded, 'Are you the party from Ireland?'

Startled, I told him that, yes, we were.

'Follow us', he instructed.

This was a hostile command, not a friendly welcome. As they led us to the terminal building, I could hear some of the others asking, 'What's happening?' 'Where are we going?' All of these questions went ignored. I began to wonder whether this was right. But then, I had never been to South Africa before. Maybe this was normal treatment. Maybe everybody on an official invitation to South Africa got this type of reception. Once inside the terminal building we were brought to one side and told to wait. I could see other passengers from our flight, which included journalists from both Ireland and the UK, who had travelled with us to document the trip, disappearing down a corridor signposted 'Security Clearance'. A few were looking back at us curiously and I could see one of them beckoning to me. It was the journalist whom I had shared a lengthy chat with on the plane.

'Hey, are you guys okay?' The concern on his face worried me somewhat.

He began to make his way over to me when two soldiers quickly intervened and ushered him off in the other direction. Their action was decisive and physical, without any verbal engagement. I glanced around at the others and knew we were all thinking the same thing – something very strange was going on.

'We are on an official invitation here,' Karen told the soldiers, while I rooted through my handbag for the paperwork to prove it.

I detected a small quiver in Karen's voice and wondered if the soldiers had noticed it too. One of them, an officer maybe, as he was older than the rest, took the paperwork and after glancing at it, showed it to a couple of the others. They were now in deep discussion and for the first time since we had landed it seemed that somebody was actually listening to us. They looked over at us numerous times while scrutinising the paperwork, as we anxiously studied their faces for any clue of an answer. That's when I noticed that one of them was sniggering. The others then joined in, their laughter conveying a feeling of doom. Everyone else from our flight had now disappeared and, as my eyes flicked around the room lined with military, it felt as though the blood had drained from my body. Their guffawing ignited raw panic in my brain as the realisation of our situation sank in. We were in trouble, just how bad I wasn't sure but as I looked around at the others it was obvious they felt the same. No wonder the soldiers laughed at the paperwork we had handed them. We were not here on an official invitation from the South African apartheid government – we were in South Africa on an invitation from the greatest opponent of their regime, a man who at every given opportunity compared their methods to Nazism.

A firm order now came for us to follow them. None of us said anything. With trepidation and in silence, we obeyed. They escorted us up one flight, then another and, as we marched, at least ten more soldiers joined the troop. I counted them as they led us down a long, seemingly endless corridor – there were now thirty-two of them in all, all armed. When they led us into a windowless room, a lump rose in my throat and I could barely swallow, my breathing quickened and my mind began to race. We'd all heard the stories of the opponents of apartheid rule: people disappearing, never to be heard of again, people dying in strange or unexplained circumstances, 'falling down the stairs' or 'slipping on a bar of soap'.

Nobody at home knew where we were. In our last phone calls home from Heathrow Airport, we had told everyone we were not travelling to South Africa, that they had refused us entry from London. But, for reasons unknown to us then, their decision was suddenly reversed and before we had had a chance to let anybody know, we were on the flight to Johannesburg. Sure, we had been nervous; sure, we had known that this trip to South Africa wasn't going to be a holiday, but we presumed that an invitation from a man with the international stature of Tutu would protect us. I guess, reflecting even more my own naivety, I had assumed the colour of our skin would be our main safeguard. My mind flickered back to Marius Schoon, someone else who had perhaps believed that the colour of his skin could protect his family. Now suddenly, the harsh light of day illuminated the reality that in South African jurisdiction they didn't care who we were or what our reason was for arriving in their country. We openly condemned their system and had travelled here to put the apartheid regime in the spotlight. For that we would now have to face the consequences. This was confirmed when we were served documents stating that the visa-free arrangement between Ireland and South Africa did not apply to us as we were trying to embarrass the South African government – which of course we were. But this 'embarrassment' was being treated as a terrorist activity, which made me feel ill with anxiety. Our suitcases soon arrived into the room and they now proceeded to go through these and all our hand luggage with a fine toothcomb. I am not sure what they were hoping to achieve, but the most lethal thing they were going to find in our baggage were the countless cans of hairspray we had brought for the ten-day trip.

I stared at the floor, my gaze firmly fixed on the booted feet of the soldier closest to me. The words that Nimrod has said to me back at the departure gate in Dublin Airport about not making eye contact kept running through my head. The soldier's boots were black leather, heavily soled and laced up above his ankles, with military camouflage trousers tucked into them. He stood next to me, pacing a few steps forward and a few steps back, but never really leaving my side. His boots were so perfectly polished they reflected the machine gun that he carried at his waist. Click, click, click – his finger toyed with the trigger. The sound paralysed me with terror. The gardaí who had tormented us back in Dublin now seemed like schoolyard bullies next to this menacing show of intimidation. The clicking of the gun was the only sound breaking the silence. Here we were being held against our will by the trained military force of an undemocratic regime. Them with their machine guns, us with nothing but the clothes on our backs.

When your body is pumping with fear and adrenaline, every second feels like a minute. As the hours dragged by, I wished more than anything we had accepted our refusal of entry back at Heathrow Airport the day before. We weren't allowed to talk to each other and we weren't allowed to speak to the soldiers.

A terrifying deathlike silence permeated the air in the stiflingly hot room. I began to worry about the younger strikers, such as poor Liz Deasy: at just eighteen years of age she was the baby of the group, and naturally terrified.

As more time passed my fear began to turn to frustration. Were they going to do something with us or not? Where was Bishop Desmond Tutu? He was the one who had invited us here so shouldn't he be doing something to help? Had everyone just forgotten us? Did anyone even know we were here at all? Most of all I worried about how this would end. No matter what scenarios I played out in my head, none of them turned out well.

16

'The Ten Deadliest Shopworkers in the World'

As planned, Bishop Desmond Tutu had arrived at Jan Smuts Airport to meet us off our flight. He saw no sign of us and was informed by the South Africa Police (SAP) that as opponents of apartheid we had been refused entry into South Africa and were currently being held in isolation. Tutu's request to see us was flatly refused and, by his own admission, at this point he was very worried. He knew better than anybody what the SAP were capable of when it came to dealing with their opponents, and it was evident they were making no exception for us. I also think that Tutu felt largely responsible as it was his invitation that had brought us to South Africa in the first place.

He left the airport straight away, returned to his Johannesburg home and set about trying to gain our release. I have no idea how long the SAP were planning to hold us – if they were just trying to teach us a lesson or if they had real plans to move us from the airport to a South African jail – but whatever they intended, it was brought to a grinding halt by Bishop Desmond Tutu in the best way he knew how:

by internationally embarrassing their regime. What others might have viewed as an impenetrable and impossible situation, Tutu viewed as an opportunity. Negotiations for our release were not going to be carried out behind closed doors – Tutu was going public.

His call for an immediate press conference brought every Irish and UK journalist who had travelled to South Africa plus every international journalist in Johannesburg to his home – and as far as he was concerned not one of them was leaving until we were released. Word spread quickly and within a matter of hours international media outlets all around the world were reporting that the South African government was holding eight shopworkers from Ireland, mainly women and all under the age of twenty-four, under armed guard at Jan Smuts Airport in Johannesburg. It is shameful and sad to know that had we been born black, this plea for help would have been completely ignored and not because of a lack of empathy but because of a desire to exploit cheap labour. However, we were white and Irish, and so, the Western world, which continued to trade with South Africa, was affronted by this treatment of their own. The international demand for our release was both resounding and ultimately threatening, something the South African government could not afford to ignore. The ramifications for their already faltering economic relations with the outside world would be crushing, and they knew it.

After we had been held captive for twelve hours, the South African government caved in to international demand and ordered our release. But not before each of our passports was stamped, disallowing us from ever returning there. We were all now officially banned from South Africa. Within minutes of this we were hurried across the tarmac towards the plane to get the next flight out of South Africa. As we were boarding Karen turned around and with her fist in the air called out, 'We will be back when South Africa is free.' I think that this was more than Sandra could take – she shoved Karen through the plane door, telling her to shut up or we wouldn't be allowed leave, never mind come back.

We never got to see our comrade and hero Bishop Desmond Tutu, or to visit the townships and meet the people we were out on strike for. Yet, even in our traumatised states, we knew that what had taken place at Jan Smuts Airport was probably going to be the defining moment of the Dunnes Stores strike.

The flight from Johannesburg back to London was a busy one, as the journalists who travelled with us all wanted interviews. After thirteen hours, we landed at Heathrow completely exhausted but as we unbuckled our seatbelts the captain made an announcement. Everyone must stay seated as the police were coming on board. Immediately, I felt anxious – I just wanted to get home to my family. Once the British officers boarded the plane they made it clear that they were looking for the party from Dublin. Dear God, I thought, here we go again. When would this ever end? We said we were the Irish party and they asked us to wait on the plane until everyone else had departed. At this stage, the uneasiness and fear I felt was visibly and verbally expressed by all of the strikers. What was going on? The officer proceeded to tell us that there was a massive media presence inside the airport and they had been requested to keep us back for our own safety. I couldn't believe it. This was a unique opportunity, one we had to utilise to the maximum. In what can only be described as a 'Tutu moment' we decided that the press conference would not be held in London, but back in Dublin – the place where our strike had started nearly a year beforehand.

While there had been about ten or twelve journalists on the flight back from South Africa, the plane to Dublin was bursting at the seams with reporters and the mood was electric. Any exhaustion I had felt evaporated in the charged atmosphere as I prepared for what was ahead. The moment we landed, Alma, who had stayed behind, was allowed through to see us. We were all happy and relieved to see her, but this quickly turned to complete astonishment when we heard that she had made some of her own headlines while we were in South Africa. Alma is tiny, very petite woman, but was probably the feistiest of the lot of us on the picket line and never took a situation lying down, no matter how difficult it was. I had always admired her for that. Just a few days beforehand she arrived on the picket to be told the news of us being held captive in South Africa, but like everyone else, she was given no further information as to what was being done by our government to bring a speedy end to this critical situation. She then got wind that our then Taoiseach, Garret FitzGerald, was attending a nearby event. She was livid – the Taoiseach was guesting at an event, while a group of Irish nationals were being held captive by the apartheid regime in South Africa. She went directly to the opening, barged past security guards, jumped over a wall and then demanded to know from Garret FitzGerald exactly what was being done to get us home. Only Alma would have had the guts to do this.

Once we were through the security gates Brendan Archbold introduced us to the world's press as 'The ten deadliest shopworkers in the world' and at once the whole room broke into laughter. In that moment, as hilarity broke out, I realised that, although I had just been through the most terrifying experience of my life, what had happened to us in South Africa was almost comical. Many years later, after apartheid had been abolished and Desmond Tutu had become the Archbishop Emeritus of Cape Town, he was asked what he thought about the Dunnes Stores Strikers' experience at the hands of the South Africa Police. Having met Tutu, I knew that he was someone who smiled and laughed a good deal, and he greeted this question with spontaneous laughter. In his opinion, the apartheid government and the South African Police had made many idiotic moves during their reign but, of all of them, this was probably one of the stupidest. To hold a small group of young shopworkers captive under the guard of thirty-two heavily armed soldiers defied any logic, in his eyes. We could have been in and out of South Africa, leaving a few uncomfortable headlines to be faced, but their brutal action towards us had brought the eyes of the world on them. They single-handedly caused a level of disgrace for themselves that we could never in our wildest dreams have achieved by ourselves.

After the press conference, we were finally reunited with our families and it was only then that we began to understand what they had been through. For nearly twenty-four hours neither the Irish nor British governments had been able to shed any light on where we were or what was happening to us. Poor Mam looked like she was going to collapse when she saw me. Da, Lar and Brian had come and in this moment any residual anxiety I had been feeling vanished – at last I was home.

(L–r): Michelle Gavin, Sandra Griffin and me at Dublin Airport in July 1985 where the international press had gathered to interview us about being held in South Africa (© Derek Speirs).

There were even more camera crews in the arrivals hall and we were all still being asked questions and giving interviews. It was during one of these interviews that I noticed something. I nudged Cathryn and pointed to Kader Asmal, who was surrounded by journalists, giving an interview. Struck down by the worst case of amnesia that either myself or Cathryn had ever witnessed Kader was telling everyone how brave we all were and how he was personally appalled by the treatment we had received.

The whole arrivals hall was packed with our families, friends and supporters. Then I saw Nimrod. As always, he was standing quietly to the background and out of the limelight. I broke away from my family and friends and went over to him. As I hugged him tightly I told him quietly what I had done – I had never made eye contact. His response was to hug me tighter. We had experienced only twelve hours of the fear and intimidation the South African regime could inflict whereas he, until he was forced to leave his homeland, had lived a lifetime of this and far worse. I couldn't begin to imagine what it would be like being black and having to face this brutality on a daily basis. But I had, on some level, finally experienced at first hand the truly cruel nature of the apartheid regime and it only intensified my hopes for the strike and my empathy for Nimrod.

Nimrod Sejake greets me at Dublin Airport after our terrifying trip to South Africa, July 1985 (© Derek Speirs).

I sat in the back seat of the car between Lar and Brian and watched Dublin Airport grow smaller in the rear-view mirror. Anticipation washed over me, but in a good way. I could feel that a change was coming our way. Even though I wasn't sure what to expect, I knew that the eyes of the world were on us, and they were watching our movement, waiting for this change. I couldn't wait to get back to the picket line and see what was to come next.

17

The Beginning of the End?

Our first day back on the picket line was extraordinary. Before I had even reached the other side of the Ha'penny Bridge I could hear the buzz and echo of a large crowd. Streams of people were merging at the corner of Henry Street. I turned the corner and was greeted by a mass of people holding banners and placards, and chanting for the freedom of South Africa. Although we had yet to resolve this dispute, that day was a celebration. Ireland and her people had joined the huge surge of ordinary people around the world, demanding that apartheid be abolished and that Nelson Mandela be freed. This, combined with a desire for our action to be recognised, now meant that numbers joining our picket line was increasing at a rapid pace. When we heard that protests were taking place outside other branches of Dunnes Stores across Ireland, we felt sure it was only a matter of time before the Establishment would cave in. It was difficult not to feel a great sense of empowerment as we realised we were now louder than the people who had tried to impede us.

Within a couple of weeks, it appeared our efforts were finally paying off: the Minister for Labour, Ruairi Quinn, entered into direct talks with our union on behalf of the Irish government. Meanwhile, Dunnes Stores were remaining predictably quiet. We knew that losing money in one store was one thing, but no company owner could ignore their business being impacted on a national level. Despite the very real sense that victory was imminent, we did not allow the naivety that had so often blinded us during the early days of our strike to affect our judgement at this vital stage. If ever there was a time to keep the pressure up it was right now. We had been blindsided and deceived too many times to really trust that a resolution would happen at the pace everybody was promising.

I think that the trip to South Africa changed us all. While it was terrifying at the time, we had all come back to Ireland stronger and more determined. Cathryn, Karen and I had always been the main spokespeople for the strike but this was now changing and the quieter ones like Theresa, Michelle, Tommy and Liz, who worked as hard as any of us in the background, were becoming more vocal. The desire of the South African government to suppress our action had seemingly done nothing but allow our confidence to grow. In particular, I noticed a huge transformation in Liz Deasy – still a teenager, she had gone to South Africa a shy girl and returned home a strong, confident young woman.

This change in some of the strikers became evident during a speaking tour that took place within two weeks of us arriving home from South Africa. The year 1985 had been declared by the United Nations as International Youth Year and as part of this, three of the Dunnes Stores Strikers were invited to speak at several events during the World Festival of Youth and Students held in Moscow. It was decided that Michelle, Liz and I would go.

Ever since the groundbreaking strike led by Lech Wałęsa at the Gdansk Shipyard in Communist-ruled Poland I had been absolutely fascinated by the political upheaval taking place in Warsaw Pact countries. In many ways it reminded me of uprisings that were taking place on a nearly daily basis in South Africa. Two very different regimes with a common thread of the suppressed standing up, united, against them. The Cold War was still at its height and while this brought with it understandable fears in the Western world it also created huge intrigue about the unknown. Due to the highly censored media coverage coming out of the Soviet Union, most of what we knew came from what we read in spy novels or saw in movies. So once myself, Liz and Michelle landed in Moscow and stepped off the plane it felt like entering entirely new and uncharted territory.

(L–r): Michelle Gavin, Liz Deasy and me arriving in Moscow, August 1985.

The year so far had been hugely significant for the Soviet Union. In March Mikhail Gorbachev had assumed power of the Soviet Communist Party and immediately declared a new course of action, one that would mark a change of the old guard and bring in life-changing reforms for many of its citizens. In a few short years the Soviet people gained freedoms, including greater freedom of speech, the press becoming far less controlled and thousands of political prisoners, some of whom had been strikers like us, being released. Although these changes had yet to play out we found there to be a sense of hope amongst the ordinary people we met, one that we suspected had not been present before.

The strikes in Gdansk and the subsequent uprisings against the Communist system had clearly inspired everybody we met and for this reason, I think, our strike was of huge interest to them. This and the fact that we were mainly women. During these meetings, talks and rallies, I saw both Liz and Michelle completely come into their own. As the days passed, their confidence grew and their ability to motivate audiences of ordinary people, who had suffered years of enforced austerity and suppression, was extraordinary. It was clear by the end of our trip that what we were doing in Ireland and what we hoped to achieve had had an inspirational effect on those we met.

A few hours before we left Moscow we decided to take a final trip to Red Square. We had been there a few days earlier and had been told that it was at night, when the square had emptied, that it came into its own. As I stood on the vast rectangular stretch of cobblestones observing the Kremlin towers and the domes of St Basil's Cathedral, illuminated by floodlights and set against the atmospheric night sky, I could feel thousands of years of history unfolding all around me. As we strolled around the square in silent awe I savoured every moment if it, knowing that in less than twenty-four hours we were going to be back on the picket line, and back to reality. Later, as we walked south towards the Moscow River, where we had been promised some of the best views of the city, I recognised that for every hardship we had suffered on the picket line there were compensations. This trip was one of them. As working-class shopworkers, Michelle, Liz and myself would never have had the opportunity to travel here. We had been on strike for just over twelve months and in that time my life's journey had been rerouted in a way I could never have envisaged. I have to admit that as I gazed at the gold domes of the Kremlin churches rising up over the red-brick walls, glimmering in the night sky, I could not help but wonder how difficult it would be to return to our ordinary lives.

* * *

Back on the picket line, it was hugely gratifying to find that momentum for our action was growing stronger by the day. With the Irish people firmly behind us we now felt bolder and more confident than we had at any other point in the strike. Actions that we would never have considered before for fear of upsetting our union or losing support no longer limited how we were willing to push our agenda into the public eye. We had nothing to lose now and every opportunity that came our way was being utilised.

On the evening of Friday 24 August Cathryn O'Reilly and myself were on the late-night picket for deliveries with a few supporters when one such opportunity came our way. It was about 10 p.m. and the shop was closed, so all the staff were long gone home. We were chatting away when Cathryn leaned back against the main door and nearly fell through it onto the shop floor – one of the managers had accidently left the front doors unlocked.

Cathryn and I looked at each other and laughed. Then without any discussion we pushed the doors open and went inside the shop. Once inside we didn't really know what to do – neither of us had been on the shop floor of Dunnes Stores for over a year so it was very strange to be there. Eventually, with no real intention of staying, we sat down on the end of the conveyor belts at the tills. After a long day of picketing it was nice to be inside and just sitting down for a while.

Soon after this a very shaken-looking night manager came down and asked us to leave the shop at once. Again with no real intention of actually doing it, we told him no, we were occupying the store. Without any argument or effort to persuade us otherwise the night manager left and we never saw him again. This was the moment when myself and Cathryn realised that maybe we could use this situation to stage an actual occupation of the shop.

These thoughts quickly evaporated when two gardaí arrived and began questioning us as to why we were on the premises. We informed them that we were two of the Dunnes Stores workers striking against the sale of South African goods and that a legal occupation of the shop was now under way. This was when the most unexpected episode of the whole night took place. After all the hostility and aggression we had received at the hands of the gardaí, we had presumed they would drag us out of the store straight away and off down to the nearest cop shop, but they didn't – they quite simply said 'fine' and then walked away. The use of physical force to remove

Much of the media coverage we achieved on the on the picket line was from unexpected opportunities. Cathryn O'Reilly (right) and my occupation of Dunnes Stores was one of them (© Derek Speirs).

Coming out after the occupation to a huge public reception and mass media. (L–r): me, Cathryn O'Reilly and Nicky Kelly (© Derek Speirs).

two young women would have resulted in very bad headlines for both Dunnes Stores and the Garda Síochána. Cathryn and I felt elated: for once, it felt like we were calling the shots.

For the rest of the night we spent most our time sitting at the tills where we had once worked or lying down on the conveyer belts trying to get a bit of sleep. At one point we got bored so took a stroll up and down the food aisles to see how much South African produce was on the shelves – there was still plenty, of course. We then took a wander around the staffrooms where I remembered back to the morning that we practised the lines that had got me suspended in the first place. After this, giddy with exhaustion, Cathryn stood outside a staff toilet door pretending to be a Dunnes Stores manager timing me while I was inside.

'Ms Manning, you've been ten seconds on the toilet already! Exactly how much longer do you think you are going to be?'

The following morning the staff and managers started to arrive for work but at this stage the front doors were locked so they couldn't get in. Other strikers began to arrive for picket duty and were shocked and amused to see the pair of us inside. We expected the management to use another entrance but they didn't, nor did they call the gardaí to deal with us. If this had been a Monday or Tuesday morning they might have done so but this was a Saturday and our supporters were arriving in their droves and the media presence was building – they knew well that any hostility or aggression towards us would not be tolerated by either the public or the press. We had by now learnt so much from the likes of Desmond Tutu and Nimrod Sejake about using every opportunity to highlight our cause that we waited inside till we could see that public and media support out on the street was at its maximum – then we came out. The cheering and applause that thundered down Henry Street and beyond was not just for us. This was a show of public outrage, a warning to the Establishment: continue to ignore us and our desire for change at your peril. That day in August 1985 was the only day Dunnes Stores on Henry Street did not open for business for the whole duration of the strike. While the financial implications of this would scarcely be missed from the deep pockets of the Dunnes Stores chain, it had done something far more effective. It had shown Ben Dunne and his management that we were getting braver and bolder, and we would not stop until we had won our right not to handle the fruits of apartheid.

* * *

Invitations were still arriving on a weekly basis so each of us, at one time or another, attended an anti-apartheid rally around the world. I think we all knew instinctively that to keep the momentum up we now had to stay local, within Ireland, or at least not too far away. The situation was rapidly changing in our favour, so it was time for us to readdress our goals in order to bring about a quick and effective end to the dispute. For this to happen we had to spread ourselves thinner on the ground and engage with the general public nationwide.

Throughout Ireland, there were protests outside branches of Dunnes Stores so it was decided that each of us should make visits to as many of these demonstrations as possible, to keep the media attention firmly focused on Dunnes Stores and the government. In late August an invitation came in for two of the strikers to go to the UK to speak at anti-apartheid rallies there, where we had been receiving mounting support from the British media since our South African trip. It was decided that myself and Cathryn would go.

We had been away only a couple of days when we got the first sign that the road to ending our dispute might not be as smooth as we had hoped. This was no minor glitch, but a very public attack from someone who had not only supported us wholeheartedly from the day the dispute started, but had been responsible for the implementation of the instruction in the first place. On 6 September 1985 a full-page article appeared in *The Irish Press* in which John Mitchell was interviewed. The headline read 'Time for Dunnes Strikers to go back – Mitchell'. In the article John suggested that the picket outside Dunnes Stores should be lifted sooner rather than later. Cathryn and myself listened as Karen read the article out over the phone and I remember us, squished into the tiny phone box, phone between our heads, weeping inconsolably while Karen cried at the other end of the line. This was one blow too many and being away from each other made it even more difficult for us to bear. The effects of lifting the picket would be detrimental and leave us with no bargaining power whatsoever, and all three of us knew it.

Once we were back in Ireland a meeting was called. During it John Mitchell backtracked on everything that was printed in the article, insisting that he had been completely misquoted. As I listened

175

I didn't doubt John's commitment to the instruction he had implemented or his belief that apartheid must be abolished, although I could not help but internally question if he really understood the totality of our struggle. This had become a massive test of mental and physical endurance for all of us. We had now spent nearly fourteen months surviving on a £21 a week. There was no reason why he or anybody else embroiled in this dispute should not have remained on full salary, but ultimately this was a stark reality that entirely separated us from everyone else. We made the collective decision to accept John's side of the story because, in many ways, we had no choice – he was our direct line to government negotiations so losing him would have meant losing everything. But for me, the trust was gone and I left that meeting with the feeling that there was rarely smoke with fire.

While this incident with John had left us all somewhat unsettled we were quickly buoyed up by the news that our action was still making waves internationally. In late September an invitation arrived for two of the Dunnes Stores Strikers to testify to the United Nations Special Committee Against Apartheid on Friday 11 October 1985, which was International Apartheid Day that year. Karen Gearon and Michelle Gavin travelled to New York where Karen gave an impassioned speech about our struggle on the picket line, our ongoing battle against the Establishment, the gardaí harassment we had suffered in the past and the plight of the millions of South Africans we were striking for. When news got back to the picket that Karen had received a standing ovation, there was pure elation amongst us and our supporters. It was hard to imagine that there would not be a lot of red faces at Government Buildings when they got wind of this news, and I think at this stage we all dearly hoped that it would send a clear message to them and the whole Establishment that we would not give up, we would not be bullied and we would not be silenced until we had won the right not to handle the sale of South African goods.

In October 1985, over a year after the strike started in Henry Street, Dunnes suspended another union member, Brendan Barron, a student and part-time shopworker, from the Crumlin branch for refusing to handle South African goods. We couldn't figure out why, fifteen months into the strike, Dunnes Stores management chose to take this action – at this stage our strike was getting huge support and the government had agreed to look into a way to ban the goods. Maybe it was a warning to other shopworkers that defiance would not be tolerated but, whatever their reasons, we welcomed Brendan and admired him for the stand he had taken.

But October turned to November, bringing with it another bitterly cold winter on the picket line where we could see no decisive action being taken by our union, the government or Dunnes Stores. We kept the momentum up and nobody could deny that on the surface it looked like we could be afforded nothing but an all-out victory, but for us, there was a deepening insecurity brewing. We were constantly assured that negotiations were ongoing to resolve the dispute, and fundamentally I think this is where much of our insecurity lay: we were not any part of them. They were all happening behind closed doors. That left us with the discomforting knowledge that any view we had might not be taken into consideration.

These fears were momentarily set aside in early December 1985 when, seventeen months after our action had commenced, the Irish government finally announced that it would carry out an investigation, with a view toward taking sanctions against South African products. They expected this investigation to be completed by 31 March 1986. But before we could begin to absorb this ground-breaking news, John Mitchell called a meeting.

It was to be held the Friday before Christmas. I remember leaving my house and Da wishing me good luck, and me telling him that I really thought this was the beginning of the end. But in my heart, I still had doubts. Everything was so uncertain. We, the strikers, had been excluded from all talks so how this decision came about or how the situation would help move us forward was yet to be revealed to us.

I took my seat at the meeting in an atmosphere infused with an insecurity from all the other strikers that equalled my own. When John Mitchell walked into the room I knew intuitively, before even a word came out of his mouth, that something was up – his lack of eye contact and his general demeanour said it all. He looked as exhausted and stressed out as any of us there but that did nothing to soften the blow when he announced that, while there would be no return to work, the picket would be suspended until further notice. This meant that if the investigation took till 31 March to complete and they found no reason to ban the sale of South African goods, we would have been off the picket line for over three months. This scenario was one that did not favour us in any way. Bedlam broke out as we argued our position but it soon became clear that this was a done deal.

We argued that the lifting of the picket could not be enforced by anybody and this was the moment we realised that we had overestimated our level of bargaining power. We were informed that any defiance of this instruction to lift our picket would result in the revoking of all strike pay. The union had already made this call and it was a decision that could not be undone.

So that was that. This final act of betrayal completely floored us. Even though the devastation on our faces was obvious, John continued to argue the point that what had happened was a good thing for us – we had won. As he battled it out with us, I just watched, thinking how much he and our union had underestimated us. Did they really believe that we had stood on the picket line for the last seventeen months to achieve this outcome, one that offered no resolution to get us back to work, one that left us unemployable to anybody else and one that weakened any bargaining position that we might have had to zero? But above all this, more worrying was that this outcome felt more like a delaying tactic than any real effort to help the millions suffering under apartheid in South Africa.

Before John left the meeting, he assured us that any delays in the government's investigation would result in our picket being reinstated. I didn't believe this.

Of everything that happened during the strike this decision taken by John was the one that confused me above all else. He had gone into this guns blazing and I could never understand what had brought him to this place of submission so rapidly. It was only years later, when my anger about the situation had subsided somewhat, that I began to take a slightly different view and this was down to Brendan Archbold. As our union official, Brendan was in the unique position of seeing both sides of the story – what we the strikers endured on the picket line and what John Mitchell as the head of our union fought against on a daily basis behind closed doors. Seventeen months into the action Brendan explained to me that Mitchell felt he had people fighting him on all sides – Ben Dunne, his own union, the Irish government, Dunnes Stores management, Kader Asmal and finally, us, the strikers. Standing by us had become too much and the consequences of it were evidenced less than a year after the strike ended when he was unceremoniously ousted from his position. These reflections from Brendan left me with the belief that John Mitchell had quite simply bitten off more than he could chew and for that I had definitely formed some empathy for him. But it remains a fact that, back then, it was his decision to lift the picket that hurt us more deeply than all the other things combined. It was he who had said only a year beforehand that we deserved to end the strike with dignity.

18

No Man's Land

The new year, 1986, brought with it more uncertain times. We now had no jobs to go to, little money and, with the picket lifted, we were denied any right to protest our position. There would be nights when I would lie awake for hours with an anger burning through me, imagining how much Ben Dunne and his management must have been revelling in these recent events. Not only was there no one at the entrance to his stores to protest the selling of South African goods, but he was also still within his legal rights to sell them. Time went by and I heard nothing. Each day was like the one before and soon the weeks began to blend into one another. We would all meet up but without a focal point it was very hard to keep our spirits up – even Alma telling us, Bono style, to 'Be angry. Don't be bitter, be angry', barely raised a smile between us. Then in February 1986, everything changed in the blink of an eye.

I was sitting at my kitchen table, chatting to Da, trying to figure out how to fill yet another empty day when the announcement came on the radio. Ruairi Quinn and his aides had completed their investigation, during which they had found a resolution within the International Labour Organisation rules and regulations that allowed sanctions against another country, if their goods depended on prison labour conditions. The Irish government had found a way to implement a total ban on the importation and sale of South African goods in Ireland until apartheid was abolished. This ban, which would become effective in January 1987, with a three-month phase-out period to follow, meant that by April 1987 not one product from South Africa would be on the shelves of an Irish shop. It took a moment for this to sink in fully, but then it hit me that we had achieved so much more than we had ever set out to. Our demand was that we be given the right to not the handle the sale of South African goods, but what had just happened meant that no worker in Ireland would ever have to handle the produce of this appalling regime again. When Da mentioned that a year seemed like a long waiting period I ignored him, not because he was wrong but because I had somewhere to get to, and in a hurry.

I jumped off the No. 78 bus, ran over the Ha'penny Bridge and all the way up Henry Street. The news had spread so fast that throngs of delighted supporters were arriving to Henry Street by the busload. We were all there, back at the picket line, but this time in victory. With the support of the Irish people behind us, we had pulled this over the line and we had won. It was mayhem of the greatest kind – we were jumping and screaming for joy and when news came in that celebrations were being held all around the country, it was one of those days you felt truly proud to be Irish. Ireland, being one of the first countries in the Western world to implement a total boycott against South Africa, allowed us to feel that, in some small way, we had made history.

Later that evening, when the crowds had dispersed and the light was gone from the day, we took some time between us to reflect over everything that had happened. This soon led to a discussion about the elephant in the room: where did this leave us now with regard to our jobs? Brendan Archbold assured us that he had spoken to John

Mitchell and the union and that it would be only a matter of weeks, even days, before our return to work would be resolved. Dunnes Stores could defy everything but the law, and denying us our right to return to work would be deemed illegal.

That night, before I left Henry Street, I peered through the large glass windows of Dunnes Stores and a chill ran through me as I thought of returning to that toxic environment. I had spent so long now with like-minded people – people who were kind, fair, interesting and made you feel better for knowing them. I couldn't imagine being back in an atmosphere where you were belittled and bullied. I knew that what lay ahead was not going to be easy. But that was the future and today was about something entirely different. I squinted through the darkness towards the till where it had all started. In that moment I could hear my 21-year-old voice explaining to the woman carrying the two Outspan grapefruits that I was unable to register the sale of South African goods today – the voice in my head was so hesitant, so unsure, that I barely recognised it to be part of the person I was now. At that moment I felt a strong arm around my shoulder pulling me from my reverie. I turned my head to see Nimrod smiling at me and it was with some pride I smiled back. I knew now we had done what he had asked of us – we had taken that weak link in the chain, forced it from a small fracture into a number of gaping holes that had become impossible for the Establishment to ignore.

The Irish government began to receive praise from all around the world on its decision to be the one of the first countries to impose sanctions on South Africa. However, this was something that not everyone was happy about. The minority voices in Government Buildings and those who had supported the strike from the beginning began to ridicule the amount of self-congratulatory backslapping going on. As the days went by the full picture about what had gone on in those closed meetings began to emerge. The idea that the Irish government had made some great discovery that allowed them to intervene with sanctions on a country that was using prison labour was being torn apart. This resolution had apparently always been in existence, long before our strike had even started and all the way through it. The use of prison labour to produce goods had always been illegal, and had always been there in plain sight. The strike had seemingly been ended, not because of some marvellous revelation that they had uncovered, but in order to protect themselves. Our action had become a national embarrassment for the government so with the flick of a pen they ended it.

Our union began trying to contact Ben Dunne and his management regarding our return to work. No meeting happened. As they had done throughout the whole strike, Dunnes Stores used silence as a weapon against us. We should have known that they were never going to back down easily but I think we were so exhausted from fighting we had lost the foresight to see what would come next: all Dunnes Stores workers were informed that they must continue to handle the sale of South African goods till April 1987, when legally, they had to be off the shelves. So, while nearly every other business in Ireland had already stopped stocking South African goods, Dunnes Stores were going to fight us to the bitter end – and they could afford to.

I don't think any of us would have suffered too much criticism if we had returned work at this point as we had, in theory, achieved what we came out to do, and much more. But we had made a promise to ourselves and the subjugated black South Africans that we would never handle apartheid produce as long as the apartheid regime remained in place. At this stage we had been through so much and each of us was so personally invested in the struggle that even touching the items produced by this atrocious system would have felt like a crime to us. There was no discussion amongst us required – under the circumstances presented to us we wouldn't be going back to work. We would remain on strike until every last item was off the shelves.

The months that followed were the lowest of the strike. Everybody returned to their normal lives and routines and with no picket line we were left with no choice but to wait it out. The union sanctioned a few pickets outside Government Buildings, but apart from this, nothing else was happening. As time went by we all became increasingly anxious about where our futures lay. Eventually we began to write directly to government officials, the Department of Labour – basically, anyone who might listen. We wanted to go back to work, we wanted our jobs – we just didn't want to handle South African produce, but unfortunately without the voice of the general public behind us, we were now coming from a severely weakened position. All requests to help get us back to work were ignored.

Our relationship with John Mitchell never recovered after he lifted our picket but we felt some gratitude towards him during the summer of 1986 when he took an unmerciful swing at Minister for Labour Ruairi Quinn. Over the previous months he had contacted the minister several times, suggesting that if the government were unwilling to offer any support regarding our return to work, would he make good on his promise of a financial contribution towards the Dunnes Stores Anti-Apartheid Strikers taking educational courses until the ban was to be implemented in January 1987. When this request was denied he released a press statement, on 25 July 1986, highlighting the continuing inaction of the Irish government:

> Mr Quinn had promised to make every effort to help finance training courses. Of course, at that stage publicity was available. But now, while other countries are stepping up action against South Africa, a self-satisfied Irish Government can't even afford a thousand pounds which is essential for the courageous Anti-Apartheid Strikers who are unable to work at Dunnes Stores. The Minister for Labour has reverted to the minimal support given for most of this strike.

While we appreciated this statement, it garnered no response from the Irish government whatsoever. One of the hardest things to digest during this period was that they unashamedly took so much of the praise for the boycott, yet provided no support to us, the people who brought about the real change. We might have been momentarily responsible for bringing the Establishment to heel, but we still needed them to get us back to work. We were effectively left in no man's land.

It was hard not to feel huge resentment towards Ruairi Quinn at this time. And while I still feel that his lack of intervention as Minster for Labour was one of the main contributing factors to the difficulties we faced on the picket line, it was only in recent years that I found out that his inaction may in part have been a result of the enormous

Protesting outside Dáil Éireann. Back row (l–r): Vonnie Munroe, Tommy Davis, Liz Deasy, Sandra Griffin, Michelle Gavin, Karen Gearon, me; front row (l–r): Cathryn O'Reilly and Alma Russell (© Derek Speirs).

185

pressure he received from his ministerial colleagues at the cabinet table. One government minister who was wholly opposed to sanctions of any kind was the then Minister for Industry (and future Taoiseach) John Bruton of Fine Gael. In a letter to Ruairi Quinn, twelve months into the strike, Bruton advised that no good would come from government intervention in the dispute and that he could not see that 'a year-long industrial dispute which has attracted so much publicity is the setting in which you should become involved'. This was a view shared by the Minister of Foreign Affairs Peter Barry, who was concerned about the potential economic repercussions for Ireland were we to cease trade with South Africa. While these details have led in the present day to some form of understanding towards Ruairi Quinn's decision not to intervene, back then it was impossible not to feel truly abandoned and betrayed.

* * *

As I struggled with a lack of money and an abundance of loneliness, the seemingly endless months tested my mental resilience. In a way I felt heartbroken, like I'd lost a close friend. The picket line had been my home for almost two years and without it I had lost my sense of purpose. We had meetings most weeks to see if there was any change on the horizon but there never was, until a meeting we had in October 1986. By this time our worry that out of sight was out of mind had entirely played out so it was suggested by one of our supporters from the Irish Anti-Apartheid Movement that they hold a march to let people know we were still out on strike. Kader Asmal's position towards us had altered somewhat since our aborted trip to South Africa, so while there was no great friendship between us, there was an unspoken truce and although he never said it directly to us, he had been very quick to sing our praises to the press.

I was apprehensive. We had been off the picket line now for nearly seven months, and with no recent press headlines it just didn't seem plausible that many would come. Surely we were all but forgotten? Despite my personal concerns, we all agreed to lead an Irish Anti-

Apartheid march in support of us, the Dunnes Stores Strikers, the following month, November 1986. While I still worried about the turnout, making banners, placards and posters gave me a great sense of purpose again – something that had been missing from my life for months now.

The day of the march came. Full of apprehension, I took the bus into town with Lar. Once we got there I could see very quickly that this was going to be a big protest – people of all ages were gathering with their banners in hand, and more and more kept coming. As we took our position at the front of the march holding a huge banner between us all, which read ' Dunnes Stores Workers Against Apartheid', the crowds, now in their thousands, broke into spontaneous cheering and applause. I don't think there was a dry eye between us – we had been cast aside by those in power, but not by the public. As we led the march through the streets of Dublin the crowd grew and grew till we reached our final destination, the GPO on O'Connell Street, where speeches were to be given. I was due to make a speech on behalf of the Dunnes Stores Strikers but first, Kader Asmal made one on behalf of the Irish Anti-Apartheid Movement. In it he thanked us unreservedly and praised us for what he described as a truly brave action.

I know I should have felt angry, even bitter, towards this man, for the betrayals he had dealt us at the height of our action, but I didn't. As Nimrod had said, Kader Asmal wanted action, just not our kind of grass-roots action. That day he stood on the podium, in praise of us, which is what we now needed more than ever. While I could never forgive his actions towards us, I respected the fact that he could tell the citizens of Ireland that our action was, in fact, the correct one.

It wasn't until I was up on the podium making a speech that the real impact of the size of the crowd hit me. There were tens of thousands of people. They were stretched so far back it was impossible to know how many. I needn't have worried about being forgotten.

* * *

Speaking at the GPO in Dublin where tens of thousands of Irish people gathered in support of the Dunnes Stores Strikers and to protest against the Irish government's inaction against apartheid, November 1986 (© Derek Speirs).

In January 1987, the law banning the sale of South African produce had been passed through and was fully implemented. There was to be a three-month period while stocks were cleared out so we knew some produce might still be on the shelves, but we had been informed months previously that Ben Dunne and his management would not expect us to handle any of this produce. On the morning of 5 January 1987 we returned to work but we were barely inside the front entrance before we were instructed to go to the staff canteen where a meeting was to be held. At this meeting we were presented with an amendment to our original working contracts that was to be signed by all of us, there and then, before we began work. This letter of agreement had only new term one condition in it – one that no other worker in the Dunnes Stores chain was being asked to sign: 'This is to confirm that I am in agreement to resume and sustain normal working on the conditions of employment that apply in Dunnes Stores (Henry Street Limited), which includes the handling of all goods that are available for sale.'

Dunnes Stores had reneged on their promise and, while we shouldn't have been shocked, we were. I can remember amid the mayhem of this meeting gazing out the canteen window down pavement where our picket line once was and wondering to myself what really went on in the mind of Ben Dunne. He knew we would never sign this letter of agreement so what could possibly be gained for him personally by this attempt to humiliate us? All of his competitors had stopped selling South African produce, the government had officially banned them but he was still persisting with blatant shows of force. We, the Dunnes Stores Strikers, had not stood outside his Henry Street store for the guts of two years because of some petty personal vendetta against him. There had been always been, and still was, a far bigger agenda at play here – the lives of millions of black South Africans suffering under white supremacist rule. Within ten minutes of arriving at Dunnes Stores we walked back out again, knowing that it would be another three months before we were able to return to work again.

* * *

By April 1987, all South African goods were officially phased out so after two years and nine months we prepared to return to work in the knowledge that this time it was for real. Dunnes Stores didn't want us back but legally they had no choice. Not all of us returned to work, but most did. We felt that that we had won the right to keep our jobs, and

Letter of agreement that we handle all produce, including South African, that Dunnes Stores requested we sign before our aborted return to work in January 1987 (© Derek Speirs).

we would walk back with our heads held high. That morning we arrived to Dunnes Stores there were no congratulations, no pats on the back – we knew what was ahead of us. Brendan Archbold came to wish us well but looked utterly devastated. I almost wished he hadn't come, for it was seeing him this upset nearly broke me. He had stood by us through thick and thin, and here he was again, like on the day it started, the only person who had turned up to wish us well on our return to work. I knew that Brendan's upset arose from the lack recognition or celebration we were getting, but in reality who was going to throw the party? Certainly not Dunnes Stores. We had been a thorn in their side for almost three years and the Irish government and our union had long since washed their hands of us.

Inside Dunnes Stores, tensions between us and our management escalated at a speed that astonished me. Not one ounce of subtlety was used in the treatment we received. Myself and Karen, who were widely considered inside Dunnes Stores to be ringleaders were singled out. Our till receipts, our clock-in times and all aspects of our work were continually questioned. It was truly relentless and keeping our spirits up became virtually impossible.

I had seen little or nothing of Nimrod since the strike had ended, but then one evening, while crossing the Ha'penny Bridge to take my bus home, I bumped into him unexpectedly. I had not seen him for months and the sight of his kind, reassuring face made me break down in tears within minutes. I told him all that was happening at Dunnes Stores, and how at this stage I was not sure how much more I could take. In an effort to comfort me, Nimrod retold me the story of Rosa Parks, the one he had told all of us strikers on the picket line, back in the early days when the grimy pavement was our classroom and he was our teacher. He told me how, in the aftermath of her stand for racial equality, she had suffered badly. She was fired from her job as a seamstress in a local department store and had to move from her home in Alabama to find other work. For years afterwards she even received death threats – all because she had refused to give up her seat on a bus for a white man.

While I was truly grateful for Nimrod's kind words of support, and knew well that my own predicament was nowhere near that of Rosa Parks, this story did little to lift my spirits in the way it had during the strike. As I journeyed home on the No. 78 bus I realised I was totally isolated, far more so than I had been at the beginning of the strike, when at least there were ten of us. Later that evening, I sat with Mam and Da around our kitchen table and we discussed my options. Life on the dole was not for me, but I had some serious realities to consider if I wanted to find work and move forward with my life.

Having been the person who was suspended from Dunnes Stores for refusing to handle the South African grapefruits, my name, whether I liked it or not, would always be more associated with the strike than the others. For this reason alone my options were hugely limited. We sat in the kitchen into the early hours of the morning and finally I made my decision: I needed to leave Ireland. By that time I was going steady with a guy called Ciaran Devine, who I had met at a disco in Lusk just north of Dublin city. I had cousins living there and during the year we were waiting for the South African produce to be banned I had started to go back there again. Ciaran worked as a mechanic but was having difficulty getting full-time work so we agreed to emigrate to Australia together and try and start a new life.

After the decision was reached I stayed on at Dunnes Stores for a good few months afterwards, not because I wanted to but because I had to save the money in order to go. But once I let my decision be known around the shop floor that I was leaving the country sooner rather than later, the heat came off me. I wasn't treated well, but I wasn't being singled out any more. I think that with regard to me Dunnes Stores felt they had won. Unfortunately for Karen, the singling-out went on until she was eventually fired from her position for incorrect till procedure. She took Dunnes Stores to court and won, but the reality remained: Karen was the loser. She, like the rest of us, was blacklisted as a striker and nobody would hire her.

On 5 November 1988 we left for Australia. I remember, like it was yesterday, being in my bedroom and packing my bags – I didn't want to go but knew I had to. I remember Da and Mam driving me to the airport, me in the back seat with Patch snuggled into my lap and watching the city I loved so much disappearing behind me. I remember Da hugging me, as our names were called out to go to the gate, and him assuring me it was only a matter of time – it would blow over and my name would soon be forgotten.

But for every memory I have of that day, there is one that will stay with me forever. As I disappeared through the departure gates I looked back, and for the second time in my life, I saw Da crying.

19

Sacrifice and Disappointment But Only One Regret

When I was very young, perhaps eight or nine years old, I remember going for a drive with Da. This was something we would, on occasion, do together if he was on a day off and Mam was at work. We travelled out of the city, away from the noise of the busy Dublin streets, past blocks of flats and rows of houses until the residential areas grew sparse and leafy green countryside took over. I have no idea where we went that day but it was obviously far from Kilmainham where we lived. We drove along some country roads, following the winding gravelly paths until we found ourselves driving down a lane which seemed to narrow the further we went. Eventually it ended at a farm gate, and as there was no further we could go, Da turned the car around and we headed back up the lane again. Later that evening, I ventured into the living room where Da was sitting in his armchair, the one he always sat in when he wanted a bit of peace and quiet, and I asked him, 'Where did we go today Da?'

His smiling face peered up from his newspaper, and he said, 'We drove to the end of the earth, Mary.'

I had been in Sydney just under a year when I got a call from Brian to say that Da had taken a sudden turn. It was a Wednesday evening in Australia, morning in Dublin, and Mam had just rushed with him in an ambulance to the hospital. The details were very vague and uncertain at this stage but I remember Brian saying to me that it didn't look good.

I was numb, but on a subconscious level I don't think that I really believed what Brian was saying to me or, possibly, I didn't want to. More news followed the next morning and it painted a picture that was much harder to ignore than Brian's guesses. Da had a blood clot that had travelled. I remember immediately phoning the hospital in Dublin and speaking to one of the doctors, who told me that, yes, it was touch and go. The next morning, Friday 20 October 1989, Da passed away. I was completely heartbroken, a heartbreak com-pounded by being unable to attend his funeral. I was barely on my feet in Australia and quite simply had no money to buy a flight home. My lovely Da was gone, the man who had stood me my whole life and I never even got to say goodbye.

In my life, I am lucky to have crossed paths with a few great men, some distinguished and recognised in the public eye, like Archbishop Desmond Tutu, and others, like Nimrod Sejake, Brendan Archbold and Tommy Davis, who quietly did their part and, in many ways, became the forgotten heroes after the strike. All these men have had a defining effect on both my life and my character, but none was greater than the effect of my father. Integrity, honesty and kindness were the traits that dominated every aspect of his life. Personal sacrifice and disappointment were part and parcel of being a Dunnes Stores Striker – we all made sacrifices and we all suffered disappointments, in different ways, but equally. Despite this, my one and only lasting regret over the action I took was that I never made it home to say a final farewell to my Da.

In the months after Da died, Australia became a far lonelier place for me. I had Ciaran, I had plenty of friends and for the most part I had settled into a good life, a far better one than I could have achieved at home after the strike. It just became much harder to be away, and much of this arose from the guilt I suffered from not having made it back and also the thought of Mam and how, in the long term, she would cope. I would phone home about once a week and for a split second I would half expect to hear Da's voice and then the reality would hit, that I would never hear his voice again. I would often think of him sitting in his armchair and wonder how I would react if I saw the empty chair now. Had I been at home, I am not sure that the grief would have been any easier to manage, but the ramifications of having gone on strike were still there, so it would be a good few years yet before I could return to Ireland.

I kept in touch with most of the strikers, particularly Karen Gearon, Cathryn O'Reilly and our union official Brendan Archbold. Nearly three years had passed since our action had ended and by then most of the strikers had found some kind of work.

In many ways, being so detached from everything that would otherwise have reminded me of it, the strike had become something of a distant memory and even though most of my friends in Sydney were Irish, none of them knew I was one of the strikers, and I never spoke of it. Then, on 11 February 1990, that all changed with the freeing of Nelson Mandela.

Since F. W. de Klerk had become president of South Africa the year before, he had entered into secret talks with Nelson Mandela. They formed an unexpectedly good relationship and, at Mandela's urging, de Klerk had broken rank with his party and ordered the relaxation of apartheid laws, the unbanning of the ANC and the release of several prominent black political prisoners in 1989 – all signalling that the release of Nelson Mandela was imminent. Mandela only found out about his own release the night before he was to be set free, so I, like the rest of the world, waited, glued to my television set, wondering what he would look like and what he would say. All photographs of him had been banned by the apartheid government since his incarceration, so, except for friends and family – and his jailers – no one knew what twenty-seven years of brutal imprisonment had done to him. The black-and-white poster I had on my bedroom wall at home was of a physically imposing revolutionary, a man in his in his prime: confident, healthy and charismatic.

I gazed at my TV screen in disbelief and wonder when Nelson Mandela appeared at the gates of Victor Verster Prison in Paarl and began his walk to freedom into a South Africa on the verge of becoming a new, transformed nation. His full head of hair was now grey and he walked stiffly, but unbent. Thinner than he was in the last iconic photos published of him in the 1960s, he now looked less like a revolutionary and more like the elder statesman he was about to become. Tears of joy ran down my cheeks when I heard the first words come out of his mouth: 'Friends, comrades and fellow South Africans. I greet you all in the name of peace, democracy and freedom for all.' But it was the words I heard further into his speech that made me realise twenty-seven years of imprisonment had done nothing to dampen his radical thinking. 'Our struggle has reached a decisive moment. Our march to freedom is irreversible. Now is the time to intensify the struggle on all fronts. To relax now would be a mistake which future generations would not forgive.' On the picket I had often wondered, if he was ever freed, could Nelson Mandela live up the iconic status that he had achieved during his imprisonment. Any doubts evaporated in that moment: this was a man still prepared to die for what he believed in and made no qualms in letting the world know that, if that's what it took, that's what he was willing to do.

There was an Irish pub we used to go to every weekend in Sydney called The Mercantile. I loved going there because once inside the doors you felt like you were at home. Every single punter in the place was Irish. And it was while I sat in there one evening with friends, sipping a pint, that I overheard a group of people saying that Nelson Mandela was visiting Ireland. At first I didn't believe it. He had been out of prison only a couple of months at that stage so why would he go all the way to Ireland? But the next week Cathryn phoned to tell me that not only was Nelson Mandela visiting Ireland but that he wanted to meet the Dunnes Stores Strikers while he was there.

On 2 July 1990, Mandela arrived in Ireland and met the Dunnes Stores Strikers but I wasn't there, and for the same reason that I couldn't get home to my Da's funeral: I just didn't have the money for the flight home. I was quite upset and deflated in the days leading up to his visit and even more so on the day, but I felt better when the other strikers phoned to tell me what had happened. In a state of total elation, they provided all sorts of descriptions of how tall he was, how big his hands were, what a warm and friendly welcome he had given them and then how, in a speech, he had praised us saying, 'Young shopworkers on Henry Street in Dublin, who in 1984 refused to handle the fruits of apartheid, provided me with great hope during my years of imprisonment, and inspiration to millions of South

Nelson Mandela in Dublin, July 1990. He asked to meet the Dunnes Stores Strikers so he could personally thank us for our action against apartheid. Cathryn O'Reilly presents the great man with a picture. (L–r): Sandra Griffin, Cathryn O'Reilly, Nelson Mandela, Liz Deasy and Theresa Mooney (© Derek Speirs).

Africans that ordinary people, far away from the crucible of apartheid, cared for our freedom.'

It was extraordinary: Nelson Mandela, the iconic freedom fighter, whose name we had chanted, whose imprisonment had spurred us on, whose picture still hung on my bedroom wall at home, had said those words about us. Towards the end of the call I remember Theresa saying it was so unfair that the purse strings of the Irish Establishment, all of whom were there that day, had not widened enough to fly me home. I didn't admit it but it had crossed my mind in the weeks leading up to his visit, and privately I had hoped, even till a few days beforehand, that an invitation would come.

After Mandela's visit to Ireland, more and more of our friends in Australia found out that I was one of the Dunnes Stores Strikers and kept asking why I had not told them. I never felt embittered or angry about not getting back – I think I felt embarrassed, inadequate and possibly even undeserving. The ending of the strike, the subsequent treatment I had received when I went back into Dunnes Stores and my Da's death had all taken their toll and something within me had perished. Looking back now, the other strikers had got something that day they truly deserved, but that I severely needed – validation for what we had done. Strangely, it made me understand Mam's need for Mollie's wedding ring in a different way. For so long now we, the strikers, had been treated like the scourge of society, and when you are treated like this for a length of time, you start to believe such bad things about yourself. I needed to feel like it had worth, that I had worth. I was happy for the strikers but sad for myself because the result was that the confident, self-assured way I had always led my life did not come so easily any more.

After this my contact with home became less. It was probably my way of avoiding things I didn't want to hear. I did get news, though, in 1991 that brought me great joy. Nimrod had left Ireland and, after thirty years of no contact with his wife, his four children, and his grandchildren whom he had never met, they were finally reunited. Then in July 1992 I heard some more news. Ben Dunne had made the headlines again but this time for an altogether different reason. While on a golfing holiday in Florida he was arrested at a hotel in possession of a bag of cocaine and in the company of two prostitutes. Within months of this highly publicised incident he was unceremoniously sacked as the managing director of Dunnes Stores – albeit with a huge payoff.

I have often been asked over the years how I feel about Ben Dunne and if I would now forgive his actions towards us during and after the strike – the answer, which will surprise no one, is no.

This is not a feeling that sits easily with me. I have found a way to reason other people's behaviour towards us during the strike action. Everybody had their own agendas and pressure rarely brings out the best in people. I do not imagine in any way that Ben Dunne is all bad; very few people are. In fact I have been made aware that his generosity, quick wit and humour are qualities enjoyed by many who know him well. But I would imagine that he is a complex man with many sides. Sadly, the side we, the Dunnes Stores Strikers, had to contend with, particularly when we were at our most vulnerable during the latter part of the strike and upon our return to work, was vindictive, to say the least.

It was over five years before I returned home but when I did, as Da had assured me before I left, things had blown over, and it appeared that the strike had been long forgotten. But when I began to look for work I decided not to take any risks, so I omitted Dunnes Stores from my CV because in my world I knew exactly what this would mean. Again, it was with regret that I had to keep those years a secret: an action that we had all been so proud of, years of our lives where we achieved so much. Once again, the Irish Establishment had shamed a member of my family into silence. This time it was me.

20

The Return Home

Ciaran and I returned to Ireland in December 1993, almost five years after I had waved goodbye to Mam and Da at Dublin Airport. We were broke and unable to afford our own place so I moved back in with Mam in Kilmainham. Luckily, within a couple of weeks I had found temporary work.

Mam had coped remarkably well after Da died. Da had always been her rock and part of me had expected her to fall into another deep depression with the weight of the loss. However, she had sounded like she was coping well during each of our weekly phone conversations, and now that I was home it was reassuring to know that this hadn't been an act for my sake. Mam was doing far better than I could have imagined. A lot of this was down to her circle of women friends and the fact that Lar still lived at home. Mam had always been more social and outgoing than Da, so while she had to contend with the grief and loneliness that a life without Da brought, she was very lucky in that she had plenty of people around to help her get through it.

Within a few months of being home, I fell pregnant. Ciaran and I hadn't planned the pregnancy and we weren't married, so I remember feeling quite anxious about how Mam would take it. Although born out of wedlock herself, when it came to matters of the Roman Catholic Church she would always be institutionalised – at this stage in her life it was not something that could be argued with or changed; it was too deeply embedded within her. Mam worried at first, but this was soon overtaken by the exciting prospect of a new grandchild in the house.

I went into labour on 29 September 1994, but it was a difficult one, and towards the end of it, luckily the midwife realised that the baby was being deprived of oxygen, so I had an emergency Caesarean section. When I came around, I panicked, thinking something dreadful had gone wrong, but it hadn't, and Niamh, my firstborn, was placed into my arms. She was the most beautiful thing I'd ever seen and I was totally besotted with her. Ciaran moved in with Mam and I as soon as Niamh was born and, once at home, we both smitten by her. Mam doted on her, too, and would take great pride showing her off to anyone who came into the house. Niamh was a very quiet baby – she just slept and ate – and although I rarely had a sleepless night with her, Mam would come into my bedroom every morning and say, 'You stay there and have a rest, Mary. I'll feed the baby.'

My parents-in-law, Betty and Matty, lived in Lusk, about half an hour north of Dublin city. Land in this part of Dublin was very cheap at the time so, shortly after Niamh was born, we decided to buy a plot and build a house. I wasn't sure about moving so far away – from Mam, my Kilmainham home, my circle of friends in the city – but this was an opportunity for us to own our own home and, with a child now to think of, it made good sense to go. I also knew that the longer I stayed with Mam, the harder it would be on her when I eventually moved out.

In March 1996 we got married and, soon after, our second daughter was born. I went into labour on 18 July 1996 and can remember thinking that it would be amazing if the baby was born the

Mam and my firstborn at Niamh's christening in 1994.

next day, 19 July, as it was the anniversary of the strike. Siobhán was born at two minutes to midnight on 18 July, which was a pretty good consolation prize, as this was Nelson Mandela's birthday.

Siobhán was only about nine months old when I noticed that she was not hitting the milestones that Niamh had at the same age. I became acutely aware that she couldn't sit, stand or walk, which I presumed to be normal developments. As time passed, she didn't talk, either. I brought her to the doctor several times with my concerns but nothing was diagnosed. We continued with the developmental tests but nothing could be 100 per cent diagnosed because, in cases like these, they don't like to label things too early. Siobhán went to a mainstream school but very soon after she started, we were advised to get a psychological evaluation done. At the age of five, Siobhán was finally diagnosed with dyspraxia and a speech, language and global

Mam with my daughters, Niamh (aged four) and Siobhán
(aged two) in 1998.

My two lovely daughters (l–r): Siobhan and Niamh, then aged
seventeen and eighteen respectively.

learning delay. It was devastating but there was also some sense of relief that after years with no answers, at least now we had something concrete to work with. Dyspraxia does not affect a person's intelligence, but its symptoms can often give the impression that it does, and this is where the main hardship of the condition lies. Anxiety, processing thoughts, social skills and fine motor skills are just a few of the challenges that are suffered on a daily basis. It was often heartbreaking to witness, particularly when Siobhán was younger. What had come so easily for Niamh – simple, everyday stuff like getting dressed and tying shoelaces – was a huge challenge for her.

We have always been completely open about Siobhán's condition and I think that this has helped both her and us, as a family, to manage it. Siobhán is now in her twenties and attends the National Learning Network, which has seen her take massive strides. She is also a member of a club, called Connections, where I volunteer as a leader, that welcomes people who are not always accepted by society or who don't fit the narrow mould of what is perceived as normal. It has been hugely rewarding to witness someone like Siobhán, who doesn't always fit in, come out of their of shell and make new friends in this more understanding environment.

In 2006 Ciaran and I separated, which brought a period of upheaval into our lives. We had both gone into the marriage with the best of intentions but, for us as a couple, it unfortunately did not work out. Luckily, the separation was amicable and the upheaval was short-lived. I remained in the house we built, while Ciaran got a place not far from us so he could be close to Niamh and Siobhán. We both moved on and met other people, and I have now been with my partner, David Keane, for over ten years.

Mam moved to Rush, close to where I lived, in 1997 and lived out the rest of her life surrounded her family and friends. She was very content and happy in her older years, and although she still talked about Mollie, it was always in a positive light. In fact, since the wedding band had arrived, bringing about her subsequent recovery, I never once saw her go low about her mother again. But, health-wise, her last two years were a struggle. She was diagnosed with congestive heart failure and much of her final few months were spent in hospital. On Christmas Eve 2011, Mam passed away. She had been put on morphine the day beforehand and never regained consciousness again from that evening. Myself, Brian and Lar took turns to make sure that at least one of us was always beside her – David and myself sat with her through that last night. As I squeezed her hand gently to assure her that someone was with her, I found myself talking to Dave about things I had not thought of for many years. Telling him stuff about Mollie and Mam that I had chosen to forget. On the eve of Mam's death, no matter how hard I tried to keep these memories at bay, they kept resurfacing, refusing to go away. With one hand clutched into Mam's hand and the other into Dave's, that night was the first time I ever shared details of my Mam's story with anybody outside of our family.

In the wake of Mollie's death and over the subsequent years I had found out more about the circumstances of Mam's birth. Mollie had given up Mam the day she was born – she had been forced to. I had also discovered that Mollie had never officially named Mam. I am sure that given the chance she would have, but this was most likely a privilege an unmarried mother was denied back then. I had found this out quite by accident when applying for Mam's passport a few years beforehand. Her birth had been registered a week after her birth as 'Baby Madigan'. Mam's claim that Mollie had refused to sign her adoption papers was also untrue. Again, quite by accident, during a totally unconnected conversation, I had found out that adoption was not legalised in Ireland till 1952. Before this, all babies of unmarried mothers were either placed in mother-and-baby homes or, like Mam, were sent to somewhere like the industrial school in Goldenbridge. These had all been unwanted, sordid discoveries that I had pushed to the back of my mind and never discussed with Mam. There had been no reason to: she had created her own narrative and I was not going to deny her that.

But sitting with her, knowing how close she was to death, a lump formed in my throat as I tried to suppress my thoughts of Mam as a little girl in an industrial school, notorious for its abuse towards the children its care, being shoved from one family to another, never knowing how long she would be in one place or where she might be sent to next. I could only imagine that her claims that Mollie had named her and that she was always hoping to come back for her were little lies that Mam had conjured up in her head during her abandoned childhood. Maybe they started as little lies made up by a girl who woke each day hoping that today might be the day her mother came to claim her. Maybe when they met in later years Mollie went along with the lies, wanting to give Mam some form of comfort, considering she would never claim her as her own.

I had, over the years, formed a far more sympathetic view of Mollie – the revelations of exactly how unmarried mothers and their babies were so brutally and shamefully treated had helped me to understand that her suffering was as great as my mother's. Mollie had carried Mam for nine months and then, on the same day she had given birth, her newborn baby was taken away from her. She was sent home with nothing but memories of what she had left behind – her body an empty sack, her mind filled with what could have been. The loneliness and pain she must have endured in the years that followed must have been unbearable, all most likely suffered in silence. Mam was a victim of time and circumstance, but so was Mollie. I recalled my initial days cradling my firstborn, Niamh, and those first cherished moments of love so strong and unconditional and the joy this new experience brought me. That night I allowed myself to trek over the broken bones of Mam and Mollie's relationship and my heart broke for both of them, for the senseless and cruel fate that had been forced on them. In another era, another life, they would have had a different story, but the cruelty of the times they lived in left not one, but two women, deprived of a love that would never be.

Brian came the next morning at about 10.30 a.m. to relieve me, and I left Mam at about 11 a.m. as I had to wrap Christmas presents for the girls. I was gone less than two hours when I got the call to come straight back in, but by the time I got there, she was gone. Mam had passed away ten minutes beforehand with Brian by her side. While I was devastated I hadn't made it back in time, as was Lar, we were comforted by the fact that she had left this world knowing that she was deeply loved and hugely appreciated by all of us. She had been a kind, protective and loving mother and grandmother, who would have given her life for any one of us.

I was also consoled by the fact that in her final days, the deeply religious stance that she had taken in her life would have been of great comfort. Mam left this world with the firm belief that she would be reunited with my Da.

When Mam passed away on Christmas Eve 2011 she left her engagement ring to me, which has her mother Mollie's wedding band melted into it. This ring will always remain my most precious possession, because Mam fought so hard for the right to own it, and it serves as the greatest reminder that my mother, Josephine Manning, was the bravest woman I have ever known.

21

Finding My Voice Again

We, the strikers, have always kept in touch throughout the years that have passed since we circled the pavement of Henry Street. I see some more than others, but there was a bond created between us during the two years and nine months of the strike action that can never be broken. We have a shared history, both joyous and painful, a history that formed part of who we are now and so we will always be intrinsically connected.

On pivotal anniversaries, there would usually some minor media attention, and while I loved the opportunity to be reunited with the strikers, I felt reconnecting with the action sometimes brought with it a feeling of unease. I was, and still am, deeply proud of our action, and have never regretted one day of it. But there was still a fragmented part of me that felt it was something to hide, something you could be branded negatively for. I hated feeling this way, but the treatment of myself and the strikers following the strike signalled that this was not something to voice proudly. That strength I had in the days of the strike, the conviction with which I spoke, I'd somehow lost along the way.

In time, though, any media attention of the strike dwindled away to nothing, so in my mind the Dunnes Stores Strike had become buried history, living only in the memories of those who took part in it. That was until 5 December 2013.

That year, 5 December was on a Thursday. I was in the car, driving Siobhán home, when the evening news bulletin announced that Nelson Mandela had passed away. I remember feeling an aching sorrow, mainly because this man had not only been my lifelong hero but because he was an icon of hope for what people could achieve. But as well as this, somewhere in the recesses of my mind, I had also always harboured a small hope that I might one day meet him. At 7 a.m. the next morning my phone rang incessantly, with everybody wanting media interviews. I was taken aback. This level of interest in the strike was something that had only ever happened at the height of our action. I phoned a few of the other strikers only to find out it was exactly the same for them. By mid-morning, I was in work preparing to do a phone interview with our national broadcaster, RTÉ. Before we even went live on air a request came through for me to appear on *The Late Late Show* that evening. I have to admit the thought of doing this alone, without the others, weighed me down with nerves. I must have given hundreds of interviews, possibly more than a thousand, during the time of our action, but that was a long time ago. The truth was I had moulded myself into a different person during the time since the strike. I had been out of the limelight for the best part of thirty years, and I wasn't even sure if I knew how to do an interview any more.

The Late Late Show is the longest-running Irish chat show and during the 1980s it was hugely political and the programme that every household in Ireland tuned into on a Friday night. During our strike, although we would have dearly wished it, the Dunnes Stores Strikers were never asked to appear on the show to give our side of the story. Considering that, during the height of the strike, we were receiving headlines throughout the world, we always found this bizarre, that our own broadcasting network would not want to cover us. This was not a moment to let nerves get the better of me. I had to do it: not just for me, but for all of us, and for our younger selves who would have berated me for giving up the chance to speak publicly about the black South African struggle.

Later that morning it was announced that President Michael D. Higgins, some government ministers and several representatives from the Department of Foreign Affairs were travelling to South Africa to attend the state memorial service for Nelson Mandela.

Very soon after this the most extraordinary and unexpected things started to happen. It began with one simple phone call to *Liveline*, Joe Duffy's post-lunchtime radio show, where people across the nation phone in to air their grievances about issues affecting the nation. This phone call was from a woman, who, as a teenager, had often attended the picket line. Inspired by what she had witnessed back then, she made an emotive plea for the government ministers to give up their seats and allow the Dunnes Stores Strikers to represent the people of Ireland at the memorial service for Mandela. I was surprised at how much emotion built up within me on hearing someone else say we deserved the recognition to be invited.

The media ran with the story and what had started as one phone call very soon turned into a national demand. I think that someone in government must have recognised quickly that this was a situation that could result in some very serious embarrassment if it was not dealt with quickly, because within a few hours an invitation was issued for one of us to attend. While we were grateful, this just didn't seem right to any us. We had all stood on the picket line for same length of time and we had all made personal sacrifices. This had never been a singular action; there had been ten of us, who had made all the same choices, and in our minds no one person more important than the group as a whole. It was either all of us, or none of us. Brendan Archbold stepped in, and in this moment it felt like we were back on the picket line in 1984.

Brendan had retired from his position at IDATU, (now Mandate) a few years beforehand but he came up with a very bold plan, the same scheme he would come up with if we were stuck for something on the picket line. His suggestion was that we would use the one flight from the government, but ask Mandate for the money to fly the rest of the strikers over. Incredibly, Mandate agreed to pay for all the remaining flights and accommodation for our ten-day stay in South Africa. I think we all felt that this huge act of generosity was the union's way of letting us know that, while the union Executive Committee of the 1980s had failed us, the present-day Executive would not. They were proud of our action against Dunnes Stores as an employer and against apartheid as a regime and could not have expressed their feelings more strongly than by making the impossible happen – the Dunnes Stores Strikers were finally going to South Africa!

On the Sunday Karen, Liz and myself left Dublin Airport for Johannesburg. As Brendan and the rest of the strikers would not follow over until two days later, only the three of us would attend the state memorial service. Walking through security at Jan Smuts Airport was an extraordinary experience. Although South Africa had been free of apartheid for over two decades, our last memory of being there was an altogether terrifying one. There was a small part of us that still felt nervous, but there was also a sense of victory walking through passport control into a country we had once been banned from. We had returned to South Africa, and it was free.

On Tuesday 10 December 2013, myself, Karen and Liz, three working-class strikers from Dublin, attended the state memorial service of Nelson Mandela at the FNB Stadium in Johannesburg. On the way to my seat I spotted Mary Robinson, Barack Obama and Kofi Annan, and then, in the distance, I saw Archbishop Desmond Tutu take his seat to rapturous cheering from the whole stadium. As if it was yesterday I remembered the warmth of his first friendly embrace, could hear his expression of gratefulness, and felt the conviction that he had so powerfully inspired within me. At a time when so few supported us, Tutu had shone like a beacon when we needed it and led us out from our darkest hours.

The lower tiers of the stadium were filled with celebrities, dignitaries and politicians from all around the world, but what was most poignant on that day was that the ordinary people of South Africa were the ones who filled the top tiers. Unlike Irish funeral Masses, this was a celebration of a great man's life, and these people broke into song and chanting throughout it. The atmosphere in the stadium was electric, alive with the traditions, culture and celebrations of the people, people who had once been enslaved and degraded andwho could now embrace their culture and rejoice with their one true voice.

I will also never forget that day for as long as I live for very personal reasons. In that moment, sitting in the stadium, something within me shifted and tears rolled down my cheeks. Like the simple act of Mam receiving Mollie's wedding band, being in that stadium at Mandela's memorial service gave me the one the thing that I had desired for so long: validation. That day, to a chorus of singing South African people, free from the shackles of apartheid, I could feel any residual cynicism that had lingered in the aftermath of the strike physically leave me. The wounds that had festered within me were cut wide open and any poison was drawn out. I was free from the internal suffering that I'd hidden even from myself. Adrenaline now pumped through my body in a way that I had had not felt since I stood on that picket line as a 21-year-old girl. That 21-year-old had faded into memory, but here I stood as a woman, in a stadium full of the people I had once stood in solidarity with from thousands of miles away, holding my head proudly once more in the knowledge that I had not ignored another being's suffering. After years of feeling silenced, I had finally found my voice again.

The one thing we, the strikers, had decided before we left Ireland was to visit Nimrod's family in Soweto. Nimrod Sejake had passed away on 27 May 2004 at the age of eighty-three. A remarkable age to reach, considering the hardships he had suffered during his life. We were told that his wife had also passed away in recent years, but that some of his children and grandchildren would like to meet us. After the other strikers arrived from Ireland, we left our hotel in

December 2013: The Dunnes Stores Strikers finally make it to South Africa. (L–r): Karen Gearon, me, Tommy Davis, Alma Russell, Liz Deasy, Vonnie Monroe, Sandra Griffin, Theresa Mooney, Michelle Gavin, Brendan Archbold (behind) and Cathryn O'Reilly (Karen Gearon).

Johannesburg to take the short journey to Soweto. As we journeyed from the heart of the city out to the townships of Soweto, it became very obvious quite quickly that while black South Africans might be free from apartheid, they were certainly not free of poverty. The shack-filled ghettos of misery that Nimrod had so vividly described to us on the picket line were in plain sight, along the sides of every road we travelled. The people of Soweto were vibrant and colourfully dressed, but none of this could disguise the horrific conditions in which they lived.

As we entered further into the townships, I recalled a newspaper article from earlier that year, in which Archbishop Tutu said he would no longer be able to vote for the ANC, citing reasons of inequality, violence and corruption. He said that the ANC had been very good at leading South Africa during the struggle to be free from oppression, but that it didn't seem that a freedom-fighting unit had easily made the transition to becoming a political party. In a way I can understand that. The ANC were treated brutally during apartheid and it is hard to make the transition from surviving such treatment to arrive at a place of kindness and compassion for all. Humans are such fragile creatures: if we are treated cruelly, we can become cruel ourselves. As I gazed around the landscape of Soweto, I looked upon a sea of impoverished townships stretching farther than the eye could see, and I knew that Desmond Tutu, as always, was right.

When we arrived at the Sejake family home we were warmly welcomed by Nimrod's two daughters Daphne and Violet, his son Ephraim and two of his granddaughters. His children were probably the same age Nimrod was when he arrived at the picket line, while his grandchildren were in their early twenties. We spoke for a lengthy period about Nimrod and told them what an inspiration he had been to us and they, in return, talked about him and the impact apartheid had had on them as a family. For us this was an eye-opening moment. We had never viewed it this way. It had denied them a father, and their resentment was obvious: as one of them told us, it would have been better if he had spent less time on the struggle and more time with his family. On the picket we always viewed it from the point of Nimrod the freedom fighter, the valiant hero, making his family proud. We never thought about how his family were struggling without a father to support them.

For me, the most profound thing was said by his youngest daughter, Daphne. Talking about how little had changed for black South Africans in the post-apartheid era, she simply said, 'Our father left here in 1960, he found us here when he came back in 1991 and look at us now. We are all still here.'

As we journeyed back to our hotel I was filled with different emotions about my trip so far. It had begun in a haze of excitement and adrenaline-filled moments but reality can't be avoided for ever. What I had just witnessed proved to me yet again that the world we live in very rarely provides happy endings for those living in extreme poverty.

Meeting the children and grandchildren of our mentor and hero, Nimrod Sejake. Front row (l–r): Alma Russell, Sandra Griffin; middle row (l–r): me, Liz Deasy, Portia Sejake (granddaughter), Violet Sejake (daughter), Loreta Memela (granddaughter), Daphne Sejake (daughter), Tommy Davis; back row (l–r): Brendan Archbold, Michelle Gavin, Karen Gearon (behind), Theresa Mooney, Brendan Barron and Ephraim Sejake (son).

Apartheid may have been brought to its knees but in true *Animal Farm*-style, the people who helped to bring this about, the ANC, who were now in power and running South Africa, had failed to spread the wealth among all those normal citizens who had rallied alongside them. Nimrod Sejake's family were the living proof of this. Nimrod's words came back to me, and I could hear his voice in my head: 'It is not just a race issue, it's also a class issue.' He had been right: maintaining power would always mean subjugating the masses, whether this was done racially or through poverty made no difference, as long as you were keeping the majority of the population under your control.

* * *

When I reflect on my life, I realise how incredibly lucky I have been. Personal sacrifice has been part and parcel of it, but I have also experienced at first hand the kindness, loyalty and genuine human spirit of everyday people. I have watched the actions of ten unassuming shopworkers evolve into an unstoppable mass movement and I have witnessed the strength and power of what a united voice that demands change can bring. On 12 February 1965, Martin Luther King Jr gave an impassioned speech in Selma, Alabama, at the height of the American Civil Rights movement. In it, he said, 'Your life begins to end the moment you start being silent about the things that matter.'

My life's journey and that of my Mam's, Josephine Manning, is a testament to this. I am not a politician and I have never aligned myself with any political party. There is nothing particularly extraordinary about my life, except that in 1984, with nine of my colleagues, Tommy Davis, Liz Deasy, Michelle Gavin, Karen Gearon, Sandra Griffin, Theresa Mooney, Vonnie Munroe, Cathryn O'Reilly and Alma Russell, we took on the Establishment, leaving them in no doubt about what can happen when ordinary people set out to achieve the extraordinary.

The only power I have is my story.

Acknowledgements

It has taken me nearly thirty years to finally write this book and I'd like to thank some people who have made this happen and who have supported me throughout the years. Firstly, I would like to thank my two daughters, Niamh and Siobhán Devine: I am so proud of you both! You have made my world a better place and I love you both so much. I would also like to thank my partner, David Keane, for his love, support and encouragement, particularly during the writing of the book. My two brothers, Lar and Brian Manning, who are a huge part of the story of my life. I would also like to thank my friends Ann Johnson, Joan Kealy, Deirdre Wilson and Eileen Goldup. I have been lucky in my life to have been surrounded by inspiring, loving people like Brendan Archbold (RIP), a friend I will miss forever. I would also like to thank my cousins Marian, Ann and Lorna Bentley for all the information they gave and Betty and Matty Devine who have been there for me throughout the years. Many thanks to Marianne Gunn O'Connor for your belief and encouragement, and to the team at The Collins Press for your hard work – I am hugely grateful to all of you.

Special thanks to Ken Byrne, Eve Buckley, Peter O'Brien, Catherine O'Brien, Katie O'Brien, Ben Buckley, Cara Loftus, Alison Walsh, Irene Connor, Siobhan Phillips, Ger Crowley, Janice Crowley, Paquita Rogers and the Tyrone Guthrie Centre.

Very special thanks to Derek Spiers for taking all those fantastic photos through the years of the strike and allowing us to use them in the book and to Sinéad O'Brien who has done a fantastic job in telling the story.

Last but definitely not least, thank you to the rest of the Dunnes Stores Strikers – Alma, Cathryn, Karen, Liz, Michelle, Sandra, Theresa, Tommy and Vonnie. You will always be a huge part of my life and I am honoured to know you all.